Praise for *Head to Heart*

"Madson captures the heart of the simple. These daily thoughts can emphatically change any moment in anyone's life. Each day's suggestion is captured in the simplicity of the thought, making it magical, joyful, meaningful, and doable. I loved it. All of it. You will, too."

> —KAREN CASEY, PhD, author of *The Good Stuff from Growing Up in a Dysfunctional Family*

"I love *Head to Heart*. Love. It is so much more than a book of daily meditations. It reads like a life map guiding you from thoughtful, relevant concepts to the only path that makes a difference—action. With this book I found that every day I had new thought patterns with action steps that enabled me to bring them into my life in a way that both motivates and brings me peace. All I can say is thanks for writing this book!"

> —JANETTE BARBER, bestselling author and six-time Emmy Award winner

"Inspiration, comfort, and peace of mind are within reach when you set your day in a positive direction by reading Jenifer Madson's *Head to Heart*. In only minutes, you will transform your day and your experience by absorbing these uplifting, energizing passages. Powerfully compelling!"

> —DEBBIE PHILLIPS, founder, Women On Fire

Head to Heart

Head to Heart
Mindfulness Moments for Every Day

JENIFER MADSON

Conari Press

First published in 2014 by Conari Press, an imprint of
Red Wheel/Weiser, LLC

With offices at:
665 Third Street, Suite 400
San Francisco, CA 94107
www.redwheelweiser.com

ISBN: 978-1-57324-598-2 *5417 9881*   *07/14*

Library of Congress Cataloging-in-Publication Data available
upon request.

Cover design by Jim Warner
Cover photograph: aspen leaves(Populus tremuloides) on the forest
floor © Exactostock / SuperStock
Interior by Maureen Forys, Happenstance Type-O-Rama
Typeset in Adobe Caslon Pro and Futura Pro

Printed in the United States of America.
EBM

10 9 8 7 6 5 4 3 2 1

To my incomparable teacher,
Venerable Khenchen Thrangu Rinpoche,
and all the sages and saints before you and
after, for your wisdom, light, and love for
all sentient beings.

A Daily Awakening: Meditations for Life

"Awakening" isn't a one-time occurrence, although moments of clear realization can feel quite sudden.

Awakening is a process; a gradual awareness; a growing insight which must be cultivated to be sustained.

Awakening to a new idea or way of being is usually a mixture of poetic consideration and practical application.

This is the practice of meditation: taking your awareness of the countless workings of everyday life from your head to your heart and then—no matter how joyful or painful they may be—embracing them and growing from them all.

It is an extraordinary practice, whether you seek to create a deeper connection with the higher power of your understanding, to generate more compassion or love, to better understand your mind and surroundings, to find answers to specific challenges, or all of the above.

And this practice can happen anywhere, at any time: on the mat or on the move, while sitting or walking, in silence or conversation, alone or with a group. In short, whenever or wherever you are consciously pointing your mind toward greater clarity and service while connecting with Spirit you are meditating and preparing to awaken.

This book not only provides points for meditation and awakening, but also questions and suggestions that will inspire you to take specific actions to grow in love and usefulness, creating an unshakable sense of well-being with which to meet all of life's demands.

Head to Heart

1 Celebrating Friendship

Few things in life are as precious as a true friend, the one who always sees what is good and possible in you and for you, who lifts you up while keeping you grounded, who can tell you hard truths without tearing you down.

Make time to celebrate such a friend: Call or write to one of them, and acknowledge a specific difference they have made in your life.

Take it one step further, and tell them how their support will positively affect your future.

Give your friend a very special gift by specifically telling them how they've impacted your life. The better they know just how they've helped you, the better able they are to do the same for others.

2 Finding Compassion

When compassion is present, there is no room for condemnation, anger, or confusion.

Think of someone you are angry with, someone you often find yourself judging or criticizing.

As you think of them, replace your feelings of frustration with statements of compassion, such as, "I am willing to understand this person even if I don't agree with them, and I wish them every happiness."

Think, write, or say these things over and over, until the anger and judgment dissolve and are replaced with a sense of empathy.

Compassion is the perfect space in which to cultivate kindness and understanding; there is no better principle on which to rest your mind.

3 Exercising Patience

Sit comfortably and begin to breathe naturally, not forcing the depth or pace of your breath.

After a moment, as you breathe in, imagine your capacity for patience, tolerance, and understanding growing as your lungs expand.

Then, imagine your frustrations leaving as you exhale.

Continue this until you feel completely relaxed and composed.

Consciously breathing in this way literally "clears the air" by calming your nerves and balancing your thoughts. This is the place from which to respond rather than react, making you of greatest benefit to all concerned.

Practice patience, tolerance, and understanding, not for the sake of temporary relief in the face of another trial, but so they may become your code, making you of better service to all.

4 Inviting Abundance

We live in a crazy world, one that seems pretty intent on having its own way for its own sake. It is easy to get caught up in that rush, to find ourselves grasping to get "our share." When we give in to such selfishness, we suppose a limit on abundance and create a mindset based on nothing but fear, blocking our connection to the vast resources that surround us.

Scarcity sounds like: "There isn't enough . . ."

Abundance sounds like: "There is more than enough . . ."

Scarcity feels small, constricted, and helpless.

Abundance feels vast, expansive, and magnanimous.

Scarcity looks at all the problems of the world.

Abundance looks at all the solutions in the world.

To see abundance we must be abundant—abundantly positive, loving, generous, and hopeful in our thoughts, language, and actions.

Help others do the same, and watch this sense of abundance multiply and magnify until you can no longer believe in anything but.

5 Finding Your Breath

Sometimes we steel ourselves against the world by literally holding our breath, as if doing so keeps us safe in the face of uncertainty. In reality, it increases our anxiety by literally cutting off the oxygen our brain so desperately needs to function properly.

Take several minutes to connect your breath to each of your five senses. See it in your mind's eye, smell it, taste it, hear it, and touch it, one at a time until you feel the amazing support that your breath brings to all aspects of your being.

Carry the awareness of your breath into the day, and reconnect with the above exercise to calm your mind and body as needed, letting your breath work with you and for you.

6 The Power of Focus

Once you make the connection between the power of your focus and determination and what manifests in your life, you can intentionally cultivate an extraordinary ability to influence your future for the better.

Ask yourself:

What dreams have come true in my life as a result of my focus and efforts?

What else do I dream of having, doing, or being?

What actions will I take today to bring these new dreams to life?

Dreams become reality through a series of countless small decisions and actions; success rarely, if ever, happens in one fell swoop.

The biggest action you will take to make your dreams come true is resolving to get them out of your head, on paper, and on the move.

7 To Be Amazed

We are surrounded by goodness, by beauty and love and spirit, in us and around us.

We don't have to look as hard as we may think to find it; we may simply need to open our hearts enough for it to find us.

Be amazed.
Be wondrous, loving, and full of gratitude.
Be captivated by the possibilities that surround you.
Be you, in all your amazing glory.

8 Quietude

We no sooner wake up before we put ourselves in high gear, careening from one request or stimuli to the next, hopeful that our decisions will lead us to our desired end.

Instead, start the day in silent reflection; create sacred time in which to plan with a clear and unhurried mind.

Find a time in the morning when you can sit in complete silence, with no TV, Internet, phones, or people to distract you.

Connect with your body: What does it need? Would you benefit from a little stretching, a brisk walk, or maybe a relaxing massage?

What about your mind—do you need inspiration, intellectual stimulation, or perhaps to organize your thoughts around the day's duties?

Most importantly, what is the spiritual connection you need to lift your soul?

The day has dawned, full of promise; now is the time to set the tone and pace of how you will move through it. You're less likely to have to start your day over if you get off on the right foot from the beginning.

9 Relinquishing Control

The act of trying to manipulate people, circumstances, and outcomes is nothing more than an attempt to create the illusion of interior calm and safety from the delusion of exterior control.

It happens when we lose confidence in our ability to handle uncertainty.

We forget that we are adept, nimble, strategic beings, full of skills and resources and answers. When we remember these things, we loosen our grip and lighten the tension and heaviness of heart that causes us—and others—such great suffering.

10 Being Playful

It is so easy to get trapped in the seriousness of being an adult and forget how to play.

Sing, dance, write, paint, act, sculpt, draw, take pictures—whatever fires your imagination and opens your creative mind.

Play, not for any other reason except that you can.

11 In Service

We make a positive difference, more than we know, in some of the most unlikely ways, simply by our determination to do so.

You don't have to try and save the whole world; save your part in it.

You may not know how to do that; don't let that stop you from finding out.

Ask yourself, "How can I best engage my time and talents for the sake of helping another?"

Don't overcomplicate it; your desire to simply bring hope to the world has more of an impact than you know.

In this process, you will find that there is nothing quite as energizing as the aim to serve humanity in some way.

12 Accepting Generosity

The next time a close friend offers to help you, openly accept their kindness and generosity, their praise or their care, without reservation.

Say "thank you," and mean it, whether or not you agree. Let what they see in you radiate through you to those around you.

Allow their generosity, and commit to paying it forward. Take it all in, that you may better pass it on.

There is no sense downplaying or turning away from the acknowledgments of those dear to you; these people are part of your network of love and solutions.

13 Go Easy

There is no need to make a mad dash through the day.

The next time you notice yourself rushing, slow down, take a deep breath, and learn to move with ease and grace.

Try to:
Walk with purpose, not panic.
Soften your tone of voice.
Slow your speech; be calmly articulate.
Smile more; worry less.

14 Asking for Help

There is life-changing power in learning to ask for help.

Our challenge is to commit to doing so before a crisis, free of shame, and to be determined to live in the solution and then share the lesson.

What help would you ask for if you had no fear of asking?

How would your life improve as a result of receiving this support?

Who would benefit from the example you set in asking, and the shift you experience from doing so?

Now that you have a great vision for what's possible by reaching out, where, how, and with whom will you do so?

15 "Terminal" Uniqueness

All of us are special in some way, yet none are truly unique.

You don't really want to be painfully unique anyway; if your "stuff" were something no one on the planet had ever seen before, who would have a solution?

You do want to feel special, though—to be seen, heard, understood, and cared for—you just may have a funny way of asking for all of that when you're trapped by your own limited vision of your suffering.

And maybe you're keeping yourself stuck there because it's the only way you know of at present to get attention (even if it's not the kind you really want).

To get unstuck, try expressing that exact truth to someone by saying, "I'm feeling like I'm the only one with this particular trouble, and part of me is keeping myself stuck because I don't know how to ask for what I really want, which is to be seen, heard, understood, and cared for right now."

The odds are really good that with that much honesty, someone is bound to step up and support you.

We are never at a loss for support; we are only at a loss for the words to enlist it.

16 Finding Humility

When you are shocked by another's "failings," it simply means you've forgotten your own.

We have all done things we aren't particularly proud of, driven by a hundred forms of fear, insecurity, and selfishness.

Knowing this, rather than allowing someone else's bad behavior to frustrate you, work to better understand the root of their suffering—not the effects—and how you might help to relieve that.

Shift your language as well. Every time you find yourself saying "I can't believe . . ." in the face of someone's shortcomings, change the language to "I understand how . . ." and commit to either being helpful or, at the very least, detaching from them with love.

Find humble, sincere gratitude for the progress you've made with your own defects, and you can then offer compassion to others instead of taking offense; you can move on from hurt instead of being stuck in indignant surprise.

17 Managing Your Mind

You can't stop negative thoughts from arising; they sometimes just do.

What you can prevent is chasing, engaging, or delighting in them.

Watch them come up.

Be very curious, almost childlike, in observing them.

Let go of the need to hang on to them.

Decide what to do in spite of them.

Find another way to look at them.

You're not responsible for what pops into your mind; you're only responsible for what you do with it.

18 Open to Possibility

Sometimes it's a real godsend that things don't work out exactly as you'd planned.

Sometimes the Universe has something else in mind for you entirely.

So organize, strategize, and prepare all you want—just don't let your attachment to a certain outcome blind you to the lessons and benefits that may come "out of the blue" or lie just outside your well-laid plans.

Embrace surprise.

19 Being Present to Sorrow

It is a great strength to be present to sorrow as well as joy.

Ask yourself: "How can I work with pain to . . .

Strengthen my soul, not weaken it?

Find clarity, not dullness?

Find peace, not unrest?"

Use your answers to face your sorrows head-on, and take comfort in knowing that the time will come—maybe sooner than you think—when you can look back and see how much you've grown through your trials.

20 Taking Stock

We will suffer major hurts in this life, there is no doubt. Knowing this, why exaggerate the ones with little significance?

When you find yourself overloaded with petty annoyances, ask, "How do these slights compare to the worst hurt I can imagine suffering?"

If they come in at an 8 or higher on a scale of 1 to 10, commit to working through them and learning from them.

If they don't, resolve to let them go before they become more harmful than they already are.

As you've heard before, "learn to pick your battles." After all, life's too short for needless worry.

21 Daily Ritual

You can't know exactly what the day will hold, but you can determine how you will hold the day.

In the morning, rise, connect with your higher power, and be grateful.

During the day, rise up, take a stand, and be courageous.

In the evening, rise above your frustrations, let go of any hurts, and be free.

Before you lay your head down to sleep, thank the God of your understanding for another opportunity to live happy, joyous, and free.

22 Vision

Start your morning by imagining what's possible this day—for you and for others—by choosing to be focused, energized, grateful, humorous, and kind.

Close your eyes, and think of someone you enjoy being with. Now picture yourself bringing all of the above qualities to your interaction with them. Imagine how much more enjoyable the relationship can be as a result.

Repeat the exercise, but this time think of someone you find it difficult to be with. See yourself bringing the above qualities to your relationship with them, despite how trying they may be. Imagine the positive shifts that are possible for that relationship as a result.

Now picture meeting the day this way just for you, and the strength that can bring you, no matter who or what you encounter.

This preparation doesn't guarantee that the day will progress perfectly, but it's an amazing way to begin.

23 Life

Life can be difficult, to be sure, but it isn't timed to get us down.

Life doesn't know what we're up to.

Life doesn't know our struggles.

Life doesn't lie in wait, hoping to trip us up.

Life is life.

Pick one very significant and painful life experience, and answer the following:

> What did you learn from it?

> When, where, and how can you share that lesson for someone else's benefit?

If we commit to using the tough times to strengthen our determination and faith, and to help another through their trials, some good can come from even the most punishing situations.

24 Answer the Call

There is extraordinary joy in following your heart's calling in service to others.

Your calling is whatever special gift you have to positively impact the world—the one you can't ignore, the one you can't help but claim.

You know it's your calling when . . .

Honoring it feels like a "must" instead of a "should."

It's usually the last thing you think of at night and the first thing you wake to in the morning.

No matter how lonely or frustrated or afraid you are of bringing that gift to the world, you don't quit.

Even though you can't see the future, you can't imagine this gift not being a part of it.

Answering "the call" is not easy or effortless—it just makes sense. And developing and using your talents for the sake of helping others will be one of the most fulfilling things you can ever do.

25 Rising Above Agitation

Don't give in to agitation; it can push you to see things that aren't real, believe things that aren't true, and choose things that aren't right.

Whatever circumstance sets you off doesn't have to set you back; irritability is just a reaction, one you can let go of just as soon as you decide to.

When you're aggravated by some person, place, or thing, try the following:

Notice the frustration with simple curiosity, no judgment.

Work with it: Recognize that it truly has no power without your permission—it doesn't have a shape, or color, or location, except as you determine.

Don't indulge or chase it.

The beauty of an awakened mind is that it sees bewilderment as it arises, and gives you the tools to examine it in more useful ways than ever before.

26 Being Searching, Fearless, Thorough, and Honest

You don't know what life has in store for you; you can be sure, however, that if you are searching, fearless, thorough, and honest, a better you will be there to greet whatever comes your way.

Search for the truth about you and your abilities.

Be fearless in your attempt to grow.

Be thorough in your actions; don't leave things undone.

Be honest about your intentions, whatever they may be.

This is the process to the grounded you, the you that can weather the storms of life; the you that is open to suggestion and flexible to change; the you that makes the world a better place in which to live.

27 Out of Overwhelm

"Overwhelm" happens when we think:

> We are alone in our struggles;
>
> Our problems are too many, and our answers too few;
>
> The stress will last forever; and
>
> We have to meet huge challenges with an equal level of intensity.

A simple formula for moving through overwhelm is to remember:

> Finding calm in the storm is the best way to weather it (be still);
>
> You won't feel this way forever—this too shall pass (find your mantra); and
>
> You are not alone—especially if you're willing to ask for help (connect).

You don't have to solve everything, all at once.
Just solve what you can today.

28 Living Your Dreams

There is no time like the present to make your dreams come true.

If you're uncertain about this, ask yourself:

> What could be possible—for me and for others—if I went after my dreams?

> How would I feel if I never went after them?

If the dreams win, then start realizing them by deciding who can help you map your plan of action.

Every time you doubt your dreams, reconnect to the reasons why you feel you must make them come true, and take one more step in their direction.

29 That's Life

We all go through life-altering experiences, good and bad, which can be stressful, to say the least.

They can also be exciting and lonely and freeing and fearful all at once. And we call this overstuffed, bursting at the seams, little package life.

Life doesn't know of our expectations, hurts, or dreams. It's just life, with all its weirdness and wonder.

The beauty of it is that even the most painful parts of our journey can be wondrous, and even the high points have their moments of weirdness; it's all part of the experience.

The secret to happiness through it all is to take it all in, as it comes, and figure out how to grow from it. This isn't news to you; it's just something you may need to remind yourself of from time to time, especially in the hardest, darkest days.

Embracing growth is easy when times are smooth; it's when those waters get really choppy that we sometimes forget to breathe and float and let the waves carry us to some greater perspective and understanding.

As life moves on in its wild new ways, find the good news in all of it; find good news in how you've adjusted to change and maintained your commitment to bettering yourself for the sake of serving others.

Your willingness to find the good news no matter what challenges you face may be the best news of all.

30 Connecting with Spirit

Who we are in the process of connecting with some greater spiritual power—open, faithful, and courageous—is as remarkable as the power itself.

And who we can become by seeking conscious contact with this power—compassionate, loving, and wise—is also extraordinary in its own right.

It seems, then, that what we receive from the act of prayer itself might have a significantly greater impact on us than anything we might specifically be praying for.

31 Taking a Stand

Be responsible for your judgments and conclusions, and where they may lead, for better or for worse.

In the midst of massive uncertainty, it's too easy to let fear drive our decisions as though our conclusions are already true, and then go about making them so just to be certain about something.

Rather than getting carried away by your emotions, look beyond your need to be right, and instead test every theory and scenario against what is right.

If these judgments and conclusions can stand this test, then carry on. If not, be willing to take a new position.

Be thoughtful and curious, and take time to reflect and think things through so that when you take a stand, your feet are pointed in the direction you really want to go.

32 Recognize Your Potential

Don't let doubt bring such a cloud that you cease to believe in the sun.

To doubt ourselves is to doubt the Divine, that seed of pure potential, spirit, and love that is within us all, just waiting to be brought to light.

So look deeply within, and recognize your potential;
connect with your spirit;
be loving.

Find the sun.

33 Letting Things Unfold

Sometimes, the best action is no action.

Not avoidance, or lack of concern, but a simple commitment to wait, to let things unfold a bit before you engage.

Start by becoming detached from a particular outcome.

Be open-minded about new ways of accomplishing your goals.

Be objective; don't insist on being the source of all your answers.

You will be amazed at what can unfold when you give it room to.

34 The Power of "I Am"

We identify with the world in countless ways each day, but none so powerful as what we say about ourselves.

How we identify ourselves can either facilitate complete and permanent transformation, or it can keep us from ever fully realizing our gifts, talents, and ability to positively impact the world.

So ask yourself, "Does what I say about myself match how I want to be seen?"

If so, keep doing whatever it takes to keep the two aligned.

If not, identify and reconstruct your self-limiting language so that it does support your vision.

Declare yourself to be whomever you want to be, now, in present-day terms, over and over, as though it's already so, and your world can't help but to align with it.

35 Being Present

Being present means wondering more about the difference you can make in the moment than worrying about whether you'll achieve your ultimate goal.

This isn't an either/or proposition.
You don't have to give up on the endgame, whatever that may be.

You're just far more likely to get there if you bring a confident, other-centered presence of mind to the moments leading up to it.

Today, be mindful of the steps you take to reach your goals, not just the finish line.

36 Learning from Pain

We don't always have to go to the depths of despair to find clarity. There is as much to be learned in not allowing ourselves to be swallowed up by negative emotions, maybe more.

What if, in the face of whatever might usually cause you untold grief, you were 100 percent open to a new perspective and response?

What would you need to let go of?

How would you let go?

What would you lose by doing so?

What would you gain?

Oh, the possibilities.

Spare yourself some grief today by learning a lesson quickly; don't wallow in bad news if you can help it.

37 Mindfulness

Mindfulness is the skill of seeing in advance whether your thoughts, language, and actions will be helpful.

It requires that you pause before you respond.

It insists that you filter that which wouldn't be useful.

It acknowledges progress, rather than perfection.

And like any strength, it requires practice; patient, determined practice.

Eventually, you will have put so much time into managing your mind and your conduct for the greater good that you can barely imagine not doing so.

38 Open to Wisdom

Our hearts always know what's right, because that's where truth lives, patiently waiting for us to be still enough to hear its wisdom.

Wisdom comes by quieting our body, speech, and mind. When we are still, our confusions can settle like mud at the bottom of a clear lake. Our fears and doubts may still be present, but when we are peaceful, they no longer cloud our vision.

What are you wrestling with? Sit, and rather than continuing to wrestle, close your eyes, breathe, and see what arises. Say to yourself, "I am open to the Universal Truth, not just my truth."

Keep a notebook handy to record any observations that arise.

When you are done meditating, look at your notes and determine the best course of action to express those truths.

39 Thoughts of You

At times you may find yourself obsessing over whether people in your life are thinking about you. Is that because you're not certain that you're loved or have made a difference?

What do you want them to think of you, anyway? That you're cute, or funny, or talented, or helpful? If they did think those things, what would it matter?

It shouldn't matter a bit, actually. What matters is that you own those thoughts, that *you* think the world of you—not in an egotistical way, but in a deep, self-loving way.

What others think of you only matters if it helps them grow or moves them to help another.

40 Shake Off the Day

Sometimes you literally have to shake off the day.

If you've encountered stress, negativity, or low energy (or some combination of the three), put on some music, and move some or all of your body in an effort to shake, rattle, and roll the weight off your psyche.

You don't even have to get up to do this. You can simply move the negative energy out through your hands.

Conduct a symphony, play a little air guitar, or go all out and dance like no one is watching.

41 Choosing for You

Don't be distracted by what everyone else is up to or worried about whether you measure up; do your thing in service to some greater good and you will have done your best.

Comparing your insides to anyone else's outsides is never an "apples to apples" proposition anyway. No two people have the exact same motivations for what they want to do or who they want to be.

Choosing just for you:

What do you want to do?

Who do you want to be?

And, most importantly,

How do you want to serve?

Match your actions to your answers and you will find little time left to focus on anything other than living up to your own expectations.

42 Managing Expectations

Learn to manage your expectations so you're not a hostage to your disappointment if things don't work out the way you think they should.

Nothing has to cause you grief if you don't want it to so long as you are responding to what is, as opposed to reacting to what isn't.

It's not about giving up or giving in when taking a stand is the right thing to do.

It's about taking on what's in front of you with an open mind, a level head, and a compassionate heart.

We are each responsible for how we feel on any given day, in any given situation, under any given stress or joy.

When you fully accept this notion, a great weight will be lifted, for then you can stop trying to control some future outcome for your own relief and instead work to influence the present for the good of all.

43 Get Curious

The life of the curious is a life of great freedom.

You get to:

> Save your energy by not jumping to conclusions;
>
> Find humor in each experience;
>
> Feel the peace of being open-minded;
>
> Develop your brain by being open to new ideas; and
>
> Cease to restrain and limit yourself.

Inquisition stops at close-ended questions, the yes or no, cut-and-dried approach to life.

Curiosity goes to open-ended exploration, the "How so?", "In what way?", and "For what purpose?" way of thinking, which automatically opens up a whole new world of possibilities.

44 A Champion for Others

Today, be the one who helps someone recognize their innate brilliance, the one who sparks their desire to bring more love and light to the world.

Show others a vision of the future and their place in it based on their skills and talents.
Be their champion.

45 Be True to Yourself

"To thine own self be true" is not a directive for cultivating selfishness or delusion, but an encouragement for developing greater self-care and intuition, for the good of all.

Be clear about your values and boundaries and commitments.
Be dedicated to prayer and meditation so you can be directed to right thought, speech, and action.

Be grounded.

Be reliable.

Be true.

46 Shift Your Consciousness

We dig paths—literally, in our brains—with our thoughts. These thoughts drive our language, the expression of our "truth."

And these expressions drive our actions, over and over.

You may wish to shift your thinking before those paths become ruts.

Don't wait for a positive shift in your consciousness; create it. It's never too late to change your mind.

47 Own Your Victories

Be as willing to accept your part in your triumphs as you are in your trials.

Your success is not an accident—you had a hand in it;

It's not luck—you prepared for it;

It's not a mistake—it wasn't meant for someone other than you;

It's not a surprise—you worked for it.

Give the glory to your higher power; take credit for showing up.

48 Operating Outside of the Norm

Sometimes it's helpful to really modify our routine, to try something completely new and different.

It doesn't even have to be something that scares you—you don't have to jump from a plane to find exhilaration.

Just do something that challenges your normal routine: Make a new friend, try a new hobby, eat something you never have before.

It will engage different parts of your brain and your body.

It will teach you things about yourself you never knew.

It will give you a confidence that comes from being engaged, excited, and adventurous.

Go ahead, shake things up.

49 Being Mellow

Don't "mellow out"; simply be mellow in all things from the start.

You can be very busy and still be "chill."

You can care deeply and not be overly dramatic.

You can have great passion and not run people over with it.

You can accomplish great things without wearing everyone out—yourself included—in the process.

50 Tell Your Story

Any triumph you've had over adversity, any progress you've made in the face of great obstacles, any success you've had in spite of your past has the makings for a story that could have a positive impact on someone.

And there are lots of ways to tell it: write, sing, act, or paint it; tell it with drama or with humor, in color or black and white, long form or short, on a screen big or small . . . just tell it.

Your experience will lose its power over you in the telling and become a great healing power from within.

Your story has the potential to change lives. Are you telling it?

51 On Growth

Here is a simple formula for personal development:

Be willing to be inspired by another's success, setting aside jealousy or envy for their progress.

Use what you learn from them to facilitate your own growth; take the best of what their story offers, and leave the rest.

Inspire others by sharing what helped you shift.
Repeat.

Who's one person you feel inspired by? Learn from their success using this method.

52 Releasing Anger

Anger is not who you are; it's something you call up, an emotion that has enormous power to hook you in, and hold you down.

Unless it is motivating you to find a solution, anger is a debilitating distraction.

If you look at it, at its core anger has no more shape, color, or location than what we imagine it to have.

Do that: sit, call up your anger over some person, place, or thing, and try to actually locate it. Pinpoint exactly where it sits; imagine a size or shape to it, a color or density or weight.

When we look at anger this objectively, we find that it is nothing more than a confused appearance of our mind.

Knowing this, visualize anger dissolving, dissipating, and being replaced with an emotion of far greater value.

53 Connection

Loving, human connection: the answer to most of the world's problems.

Go out of your way today to truly connect with someone through a kind touch, a kind word, eye contact, and a smile.

Stop everything you're doing, and get heart to heart with someone. How about right now?

54 Into Action

We spend a lot of time contemplating change in varying areas of our lives, but what does it take for us to actually make a move?

The fact is, we rarely choose what's practical, or a "should." But if you deem something a "must," you will shift and accomplish great things in your life because some imperative of the social, relative, professional, moral, or spiritual variety has dictated that you have to.

Figure out your "musts"—

the things you must do,

the person you must be,

the ways in which you must serve—

in all areas of your life.

Let your "musts" drive you, and your life will unfold in
miraculous ways.

55 Practice

Every day brings opportunities to practice:
letting go,

growing in love and usefulness,

leaving the past behind and creating a new future, and

living the promises of an examined, purposeful life.

Practice brings progress; progress brings peace.
Bring on the day.

56 The Perfect Day

A perfect day
starts with faith,
proceeds with action,
engages with love,
and ends with gratitude.

Make today a perfect day.

57 Embrace Uncertainty

In the face of great uncertainty, find love.
Love for the journey,
Love for what surrounds you,

Love for the chance you're given to make a difference.

Embrace the time between moments of uncertainty and
eventual clarity for the priceless opportunity it gives you to
calm your mind and deepen your faith.

58 Excellence

We often put up with less than ideal thoughts, relationships, and circumstances because we don't know how to deal with them, or we don't think they are important enough to pay attention to.

It could be something as innocuous as a junk drawer; you know, the one that is stuffed so full you can barely open it, that has long lost its original purpose, that never offers what you seek from it, the mere thought of which robs you of joy?

Imagine how much more time and energy you would have for the more important things in your life if you didn't have to waste time fighting with the junk drawer, if it were restored to order and value.

Make a list of all the things you're putting up with that don't meet your standards of excellence, and begin to correct or eliminate them. Notice the amazing freedom that comes from doing so.

Insist on an excellent junk drawer.

59 The Adventure of Life

Our lives will always be a mixture of crazy, peaceful, sexy, silly, tragic, and enchanting moments, never just one or another.

Rather than searching to separate the "good" from the "bad," seek to see all experiences as necessary to the other; appreciate that you fully know joy because you have thoroughly known pain.

Look at what is "right" about what is "wrong" in your life, how the ups influence the downs, and vice versa.

Once you see all separate events as part and parcel of the full experience of life, you are less at the mercy of its whims, and more able to roll with what comes.

Life then becomes more of an adventure to be enjoyed, and less of a trial to endure.

60 Bring the Day

Ask not what the day can bring to you, but what you can bring to the day.

Make a list of how you want the day to be. Then add how you will embody each of those qualities.

Let's not wait for favorable things to happen, for people, places, and things to "do right"; instead, let's make a conscious effort to bring every quality we seek to the table from the start.

61 Here's the Thing

The "thing" is rarely the "thing"—usually it is the thing that *leads* to the thing that is the thing.

Or something like that.

We get our hearts set on certain things working out a certain way. We tell ourselves, "If I do X, then I will get Y"; "this" means "that."

But what if X leads to Z, and "this" means something entirely different from "that"?

If our happiness is tied to one version of the future, we will be constantly disappointed.

However, if we learn to appreciate where we are now, and where it might lead in the future, we can sustain our energy and focus and always have something to be happy about.

We can't predict the future; we can only hope to influence it with our intention and focus. You never know, ending up somewhere entirely different than where you'd planned might turn out to be the perfect place to be.

62 With Love

Share with love in mind.
Be lovingly present to another's thoughts.
Show love for another's efforts.

Be fiercely proud—smiling all the while—of the potential in our humanity when we turn to each other with love.

In a word, be lovely.

63 Inviting Wisdom

Sometimes you wake to a perfect storm of things gone wrong which, taken separately, wouldn't rattle your cage, but when taken together have the power to cut a destructive path of frustration, anger, and doubt.

Those are the perfect times to invite the peace, courage, and wisdom that come from determining what needs change and what needs acceptance.

Thank goodness for the Serenity Prayer, which provides the perfect template.

Next time you find yourself in a bind, remember that you can change some things, but you need to accept others. It's up to you to have the wisdom to know the difference.

64 To Pray

It doesn't matter how we pray—hands pressed together or lifted in praise; eyes closed or turned heavenward; on our knees, cross-legged on the floor, or standing over a cup of coffee; with full sincerity or "faking it till we make it"—just the effort of making conscious contact with a power greater than ourselves is enough to make us available to the pure love and compassion that power brings.

Take a moment out today for prayer in any form.

65 Cultivating Patience

Patience should be no more difficult to show than frustration; each is a habit of the mind and body.

The one that gets exercised most is the one that will be most engaged and will have the greatest influence on your life.

When you're stressed, default to patience, not frustration.

66 In a Word

Context is everything.

Take the word "projection." For many, the word means forecasting a negative future, usually without evidence to support a pessimistic view caused by being caught up in a swirl of fearful what-ifs.

For some, however, projection means an ability to exude great faith followed by action, supported by the confidence that when they step into what feels like a great unknown, they will either possess their answers or know where to find them.

Each of us has the power, before we ever get out of bed, to choose which frame of reference will rule the day. This makes your morning ritual that much more critical.

67 Detaching with Love

One of the greatest skills you can learn is to detach from the people, places, thoughts, and emotions that don't serve the greater good and to find the willingness—the drive, actually—to seek those that do.

We typically learn to detach when we tire of the "catch and release" program of getting incessantly snared in useless drama.

That drama might come from outside of us; sometimes it is of our own making.

Either way, detachment from drama is a choice and a process.

The more you learn to focus on solutions, the faster you will be able to discern—and step away from—that which is only focused on problems. It will become crystal clear that it does no one any good to buy into something that can't come to some good. And you'll know you are exercising useful detachment—and not just fearful escape—when you can step away with no shred of moral superiority; when you can do so with love.

68 Surrender to Win

What if you were to let some greater power direct your thoughts and actions, and take a full leap of faith that the victory is in "letting go and letting God"?

Surrender your ego and stop fighting imaginary battles that have no substance or merit and you gain clarity, spirit, and love.

You are free.

You win.

69 Defining Yourself

We create identities, consciously or subconsciously, that are not always a full expression of our potential.

For instance, do you see yourself as smart, and not just in a "book smart" way?

Some of us think we're only really smart if we have some kind of advanced degree in an important field; that it doesn't really count to be clever or "street smart."

But smart is as smart does—the official definition of the word includes "savvy" as well as "brainy."

In that case, you have probably proven yourself to be pretty smart about a lot of things.

In order to see ourselves in a fresh new light, perhaps we need a fresh new definition in order to break out of our old identity.

Pick a new word that perfectly describes you, or pick a new definition for an old word.

Change the word or change the meaning of the word; the intention behind the word is what matters most.

70 Being Fulfilled

If you never achieved or acquired another thing, would you be happy?

If you never got to cross everything off your bucket list, would you feel, on your dying day, like your life was unfulfilled?

There is one thing for almost everyone that is a constant, whether or not they ever made it through their list, and that is to feel like they mattered.

Mattered as in they made a difference in someone else's life.

That they were loved for who they were as a person, not for where they went or what they had.

Maybe it would help to replace our bucket list with our ideal eulogy, and focus on living up to what we hope will be said of the mark we made in life.

71 Practical Spirituality

It is usually a very practical approach that leads to a spiritual experience.

Suit up.

Show up.

Bring your best effort.

Try to work for the benefit of all.

Do that, and at the end of the day you are bound to feel the joy of knowing that you have done what your higher power would have you do.

72 Willingness to Grow

We most likely have everything we need—all the words, methods, and sources of inspiration—to grow in love and usefulness; we may just be missing the willingness to use them.

We become willing to take action when the pain of staying where we are becomes too much to bear, or the pleasure of what we might gain becomes irresistible.

Either scenario implies a point of pressure, which, when applied with great enough force, causes us to make a move.

It's up to us which one we choose.

Would you rather be motivated by fleeing from your current circumstance, or by rushing toward an irresistible future? It's your call when to act and why.

73 On the Roller Coaster

When life brings the stomach-churning ups and downs of a roller coaster, you can either grit your teeth and white-knuckle your way through it, or you can strap yourself in, throw your hands in the air, let the wind catch you full in the face, and squeal with delight for the chance to feel every second of its twists and turns.

Will you fully engage in the ups and downs of life or choose to pass on the ride?

74 The Miracle of Your Body

Stretch.

Grow.

Literally, reach for the stars,

feel the length of your muscles,

the strength of your bones.

Marvel at how your skin holds you all together.

Open your arms wide,

lift your heart.

Open your eyes, and really see what's in front of you.

Smile like you know something secret and special and can't wait to share it with the world.

75 Accepting Praise

We struggle to accept praise and congratulations for things we feel we should have done earlier, faster, or better.

That is, until we realize that people aren't just saying, "Yay for you," for your own sake, but because your progress brings hope to them and others, as anyone's progress would.

With that in mind, feel free to fully share in whatever acknowledgment or celebration comes your way.

Yay for hope!

76 In Community

We are all a part of so many tribes.

Some we are born into, some we elect, some we create, and some are thrust upon us.

Think of who "your people" are, the value of that community, and how you contribute to that value.

Ask yourself, "Would I like to have more of an impact in my community?"

If so, map out exactly what you'd like to do and how you'd like to do it, and be highly mindful of the great lessons that can be shared in the process from within the community.

77 Confidence

True confidence doesn't just appear; it is a trait you develop by challenging the perceived limits of your brain, body, and spirit, by living life fully and learning from every piece of it, and by gratefully accepting instruction, love, and support in the process.

Confidence is already within you, attached to some event or accomplishment you may not have given yourself much credit for at the time but which, upon further examination, might help you see yourself now in a beautiful and powerful light.

Your confidence needn't be gauged, as in "better than" or "worse than," or judged as higher or lower. You can simply celebrate its existence and honor it by using it to spark the same self-assurance in others.

78 Sincerity

Sincerity is a great virtue present in those who are always intent on expressing their thoughts and feelings honestly, regardless of agreement and sometimes at the risk of outright rejection.

It is a quality that cannot be claimed through mere words, but can be proven only by genuine action.

To act with sincerity is to cultivate great integrity, and to make your way in the world driven by the deep courage of your convictions.

You may not always agree with the sincere man, but you will likely respect his candor.

79 Self-Care

Self-care is often synonymous with shutting down, checking out, relaxing, stepping back, or suspending some activity so that we can take better care of our mental, physical, spiritual, emotional, or financial health.

To go from dreaming about self-care to actually administering it . . .

Pick a category to start: mental, physical, spiritual, emotional, or financial health.

Then choose a phrase to go with the category, and then map out how to accomplish it. For example, you might say, "I need to 'check out' so I can take better care of my mental health."

Next, describe what it means to you to "check out," and then list two or three things you can do as a result to take care of your mental health. (Don't forget, sometimes the best thing you can do to care for yourself is ask someone else to care for you.)

And finally, just do it.

Self-care isn't limited to bubble baths and "me time"; we need to take better care of ourselves in all areas of our life. Make that step to treat yourself well today.

80 Your Talents

It is thrilling to discover our skills and talents, and even more fulfilling to turn them from strengths into gifts.

Start by acknowledging some of your skills and talents and how they have boosted your confidence and bettered your life.

Then figure out how to use them—today—to better the lives of others.

There's no sense keeping all that talent a secret, is there?

81 Living Life

Perhaps we should spend less time trying to make sense of life and more time actually living it.

We ask ourselves such potentially torturous questions as, "Why are we here?" "Why do bad things happen to good people?" . . . Why, why, why.

"Why?" can be a great starter question, but only if we're willing to explore it to a fruitful conclusion.

Otherwise, we should probably let it go, and focus on what's next. Or how to be the best we can be, or the when, who, and where questions of how to take the next steps.

It seems that the question of "Why?" isn't nearly as important as "What now?"

82 Personal Inventory

There is something profoundly healing in using the written word to examine your life and take responsibility for your part in its events, good or bad.

Writing your story teaches you context: It shows you the relation of your actions to your circumstances, illuminating your choices in all matters.

Writing brings growth: It can provide a great visual for how much you've shifted and developed over time.

Writing is also a great outlet for honesty: When you are searching and honest on paper, you get better and better at being curious and forthright in real life.

Make some time to write your story—you never know what will surface when you put words to your emotions and thoughts.

83 Honoring Your Values

It's easy to forget our guiding principles and get caught up in things that don't really fit our values; to be tempted by people, places, and things that excite us but which don't contribute to our growth.

Are we really more interested in simply being stimulated than in honoring our ethics?

If you can find what does both, then more power to you.

And if you can also add what's useful to others to the mix, then you're really on to something.

What are three things you can do that support your values and excite you?

84 New Solutions

There is no single, perfect way to deal with the challenges of life.

And there is nothing wrong with finding new ways to deal with old struggles, as long as these new strategies move us forward and uphold the standards we've set for ourselves.

What's an old problem in your life that needs a new solution?

85 Being Decisive

Decisiveness is:

Swift, conscious choice.

Taking a stand, despite any fear.

Following through even when you don't know exactly where it will lead.

Celebrate your determination, even if it takes a while to get to it.

86 Joy

Joy.

Find it everywhere.

Feel it all over.

Express it out loud.

Generate it wherever and whenever you can.

Joy is in the world, and in us. Notice its abundance today.

87 On Loneliness

One cause of loneliness is the physical absence of meaningful people in one's life.

A great remedy for loneliness, then, is to commune with like-minded souls who are gathered for the sake of something good.

There's nothing like a group's collective spirit and positive intention to ignite and fuel one's own.

88 Grace

If you have known courage, then you have known wisdom.

If you have known wisdom, then you have known peace.

If you have known peace, then you have known serenity.

If you have known all of these in the face of impossible odds, then you have known grace.

We've all had times when we've experienced grace. Foster that feeling in everything you do.

89 Personal Growth

One sure way to know you've grown is that you find yourself more interested in rising to new standards and challenges than falling for old and limiting stories about what you're capable of.

It's not that you simply outgrow your old stories overnight; rather, they shift and improve based on your willingness to challenge them, to reach new heights of accomplishment through those challenges, and to gather evidence of your new strengths.

What we believe about ourselves is nothing more than an accumulation of external experiences to match what's in our mind.

The simple truth, then, is that every story starts in your mind.

Knowing this, what stories are you ready to rewrite?

90 Tranquility

Tranquility speaks as much to a specific physical, mental, emotional, or spiritual stillness as it does to an overall sense of composure.

Meditation teaches you how to reach a sense of calm in all these aspects of your being, so if you know how to rest all of your faculties, separately and then collectively, then you have the power to choose which combination of these aspects to activate at any given time.

You are in control of how best to move through life with serenity at any given moment, on any given day.

91 Live Creatively

To live creatively is to:

be active, inventive, and imaginative;

forge a new path;

be original; and

see the world in a new and improved light.

Lead the way.

92 Hard Choices

While you are not alone in making hard choices, there are definitely times when they are yours alone to make—yours and your God's.

No running around trying to get everyone else's opinion.

No using other people's motivations as your own.

No trying to make up reasons to not take these challenges on.

It's just you and your higher power, looking for what's really true for you, and the courage to stand up for it.
 Once you make a decision on that level, have that pure moment of truth; no outside influence can shake it.

93 Being "Enough"

There are times in everyone's life when they question whether they are "enough."

In particular, when you undertake any significant personal development challenge, you may find yourself questioning whether you're worthy of the benefits of that undertaking.

You may be a little afraid of what you hear about the promises of how you'll change, of the new dimensions of awareness you might achieve.

You don't have to just trust what you hear is possible in stretching beyond your comfort zone; it is just as important to look for hard evidence of the benefits others have experienced by challenging themselves in the same way.

Trudge along, and do the work anyway in case you're wrong about whether you're worthy of those blessings.

Better yet, prove yourself wrong.

You are just as deserving of grace and opportunity as anyone else.

94 Your Mind

How fascinating it is to consider all the brilliant parts of your mind: the creative parts; the loving parts; the mechanical, analytical, and sensory parts.

And how exciting it is to find new and interesting ways to stimulate and strengthen them.

We often see ourselves as right- or left-brained, creative or analytical, one or the other; but in truth, while we tend to use certain parts of our brain more than others, we are not bound to this pattern.

When we introduce both sides of the brain to each other, we can assign "roles" to them that support the main goal: Our creative right side is there to keep us focused on the big picture, while the logical left side keeps us locked on to completing the details.

Learn to use your whole mind, make all parts interdependent, and you will become a true force to be reckoned with.

95 The "Committee"

The purpose of a committee is to judge: to be objective and fair based on evidence, to be solution-oriented, and to advance the agenda they've been tasked with.

Why is it, then, that when we speak of "the committee" in our head we tend to characterize it as having anything but these qualities?

Sure, the judging piece is usually there, but the objectivity, fairness, and evidence-based conclusions are gone. In their place is usually a cynical mob intent on highlighting the worst pieces of our past as proof of our forever uncertain, damaged, and unenlightened future.

If this describes your committee, then it's high time you fired them and hired a new one.

Imagine the difference it will make when your internal committee is made up of the people in your life who most believe in you and your potential for greatness.

Think of it like a vision board for your mind, with people you know and love all lined up on your behalf, asking strategic questions, challenging you, and cheering you on, and your higher power as chairman.

Do you need a new committee? Who will you elect to be on it?

96 Contribution

To make a contribution is to do your part to help someone or something advance.

Your part is whatever is helpful, regardless of whether you are recognized for having done it or not.

No matter how big or how small.

Sooner rather than later.

Whether it's easy or hard to do.

Carry on.

What will you contribute to the world today? How can you be of service?

97 Connection

We have a base need as human beings to connect with others through experiences and ideas.

It is born in us, this need to relate; it helps us feel seen and alive.

The best connections are those we purposely make for the sake of mutual growth; they are mindful.

Mindful connections create experiences that move us, that expand our hearts and our capacity for love and compassion; they are meaningful.

Meaningful connections forever bind us to others who are intent on leaving a positive mark in the world; they are memorable.

How will you foster more meaningful connections in your life?

98 Dreams

Once we give ourselves permission to dream bigger than we have before, we are faced with the responsibility of stepping up to the actions that will make those dreams come true.

And maybe that dream scares us a little, so maybe we retract a bit; but chances are that once we've dreamed something bigger for our lives, the smaller vision we came from no longer fits; it now feels a little tight and restrictive.

So we step out again, maybe not into as big a vision as before, but one that still moves us to wonder, and experiment, and progress; one with enough room to stretch our limits, if just a little, if just for a short time.

After a while, once we've experienced enough of the benefits of this new vision, we find ourselves longing for more; so we either step into yet another, bigger dream, or we bring even more energy and enthusiasm to the one we're in.

It's a process, this vision and action business, a dance that takes us a little bit forward, a little bit back, a little bit forward, and forward still, and then maybe a little bit back.

As long as we keep stretching our minds and our imagination, as long as we keep them clear, keep challenging them, they can never return to a state of unknowing.

99 Self-Interest

Human beings are self-interested.

It is in our DNA, since the dawn of our existence, to need food, shelter, clothing, love, and belongingness to feel secure.

It's how we meet our basic needs that defines who we are, not the needs themselves.

100 Perspective

Finding perspective is a big choice, a grand process for reaching an ultimate understanding of the simple and relative importance of any given element of life.

It is a series of action steps . . .

which challenges you to examine things from different angles than what you may be comfortable or familiar with,

which gives you the chance to discover new ways of thinking,

which allows you to gain greater clarity, possibly putting you on a new and improved path,

which may bring you a more positive result than what you had before.

In the end, you may not come to a conclusion different than what you started with, but you will grow—in awareness and understanding—when you are willing to see things differently before making up your mind.

101 Personal Choice

What does it take to accept full responsibility for where you are in life?

Claiming personal responsibility begins when you are introduced to the concept and start to test the theory, over and over, until you cannot come to a more logical conclusion.

It happens when you are repeatedly asked—and are willing to answer—the question, "What was your part in 'it'?"

And then it becomes a credo of sorts, a personal philosophy and way of being.

And that way of being changes everything about how you come to life. It changes your language: You go from "have to" to "get to," "have decided," "must," and "I will."

Accepting full responsibility for your life changes you mentally, making you more inquisitive, discerning, and perceptive.

And the more you own your choices—the good ones and the bad—and where they might lead, the more empowered you will feel to make faster, stronger, and better ones.

102 Belief

There is magic in each day, when you believe in magic.
There is love, all around, when you believe in love.

There is opportunity, grace, and spirit in all things, when you open your eyes to them.

There is peace and serenity at your fingertips, when you invite them.

Believing is seeing.

103 On Agitation

When you are emotionally and mentally frustrated, it is a great practice to take a beat before reacting.

> That could mean:
>
> taking a breath (short or long),
>
> tapping out a favorite rhythm against your leg,
>
> clasping your hands loosely (as though in prayer), or
>
> closing your eyes for a brief moment.

A small physical act such as one of these will create a pause and give you time to gather your thoughts and direct them toward a more useful end.

104 Living

Your life is yours to live.

Live it wisely,

live it with gusto,

live it in full view of those you might help by its example.

Live it with gratitude, grace, and curiosity.

Live it up.

105 The Path to Peace

The quickest route to peace, serenity, and acceptance is through your mind; you begin by inviting these qualities into your life, and then make room for them to manifest by being willing to embody them in the face of whatever life brings you.

From that willingness you can then progress to using any number of tools to employ them.

Breathing, smiling, generating compassion, and expressing empathy are just a few of the tools that will transform peace, serenity, and acceptance from a way of thinking to an ingrained way of being.

106 Your Ultimate Outcome

The difference between being alive and truly living lies in our ability to articulate and carry out our ultimate outcome for any particular facet of our being.

Take a careful look at the main categories of your life—your physical, mental, emotional, spiritual, and financial aspects—and ask yourself, "Am I living on purpose, or just poking around the edges of what's possible?"

Chances are you want to live more deliberately in at least some of these areas. You simply need to better define exactly what that means to you. So do this—write out your ultimate outcome, knowing that this is your definition alone, unfettered by the pressures of others.

It is sacred, one you'll refer to repeatedly. It is your guiding light.

It is not random or careless, but an intentional expression of your full potential.

Write and rewrite your ultimate outcome until you have a version that moves you, inspires you, feels like it will rocket you out of bed each day.

107 Your Driving Purpose

The source of energy for pushing through to your ultimate outcomes in life is the "whys"; the myriad of payoffs you can perceive for doing what you do.

You have identified what it is that you really, really want by articulating these outcomes; now it is imperative that you look at your reasons for achieving them.

No matter how big or how small, your "whys" fuel your will. So whenever you engage with what you really want, be sure to tap into exactly why this goal matters. Because when your resolve falters on the way to your goal, what you set out for won't inspire you to continue nearly as powerfully as why you choose to pursue the goal in the first place.

What are your "whys" for doing what you do?

108 The Map to Your Mission

If you want to go from just being busy to being fully engaged with life, ditch the to-do lists and replace them with to-love, to-live, and to-serve lists.

This simple shift will help you feel more fulfilled in the process of completing action items, because now you'll be following a well-designed plan to reach some significant mission, instead of just checking off a bunch of tasks that don't add up to much.

Even making the bed becomes less mundane when it's on a to-live list that is tied to the ultimate outcome of creating a sacred space for rest and renewal.

109 Commune with God

The closer you get to God (whatever your concept of God), the nearer you are to your solutions.

The nearer you are to your solutions, the less time you will spend in problems.

The further you are from living in the problem, the fewer of them you will have.

As a meditation, picture yourself side by side with whatever higher power you believe in. Allow yourself to be filled with the spirit of that power with each breath you take, supported by infinite love and grace, and as you exhale, give all your troubles over to this great source of all solutions.

Ask for answers as you breathe in. Let go of your fears as you breathe out.

Open your mind to the answers that arise, and end your meditation with the willingness to put them in action.

Find answers through meditation and communing with the God of your understanding.

110 Know Thyself

You can't be true to yourself unless you really know yourself, with all your talents and limitations, your confidences and fears, where you shine and where you need to improve, what moves you and what slows you down, what you value and what you don't.

You must know yourself in reference to your past and your present to know what's possible for your future.

The great news is, you don't need to know it all at once.

You can tell what you don't know about yourself when you encounter something that bewilders you, some situation that truly gives you pause.

In those times, you must explore what confuses you in order to discover what it means to be true to yourself in that case.

111 Intentional Growth

You intuitively know what you need to grow in love and service; ask for it, and keep asking until you either get help from outside yourself or find your answers and resources from within.

Be relentless, and determined to grow.

112 Rest

Stop everything else and sit, breathe, and refresh your spirit, if only for a short time.

It's not so hard to do; we crave it, really.

Understand that even the briefest moments of intentional serenity can make a vast difference to how we approach the rest of the day.

113 Impact First

The ultimate proof of your spiritual commitment is the willingness to manage your mind and your conduct for the benefit of all, with the ultimate faith that you will be cared for in the process.

It's a lofty goal, for sure.

It is certainly one worth shooting for, though, because if we condition ourselves to pause before speaking, to think things through and choose actions that will be most helpful for all concerned, we will not only individually effect great change, we will also set a great example for others to do the same.

Think first, act second, and act from impact rather than impulse.

114 Choose Your Principles

Choose your principles. For life, love, family, friendships, work, play, and service.

Some of them may be very familiar and ingrained in you already; some you may be trying on for the very first time.

Either way, practice them in all your affairs until they become forever woven into the fabric of your life.

Until you can't imagine life without them.

Today is the perfect day to clearly articulate what matters to you most.

115 Your Missions

Your missions are the things that everyone knows you're "about." It's the stuff we admire about you. Even those who don't know you well know your missions.

If you're not sure today how to articulate your missions in life, just ask someone who knows you well to help you clarify and define them.

116 Finding the Good

We are asked to see the good in people, but sometimes we're only willing to do so when we think they are worth seeing in a better light.

What about the most awful people you can imagine, the ones who have done great harm to the world? How do you find the seed of goodness in them, and, for gosh sakes, why would you even try?

Do it because if you try to find value in someone who seems devoid of any, even if you can't find it, your willingness to try helps you develop a level of compassion and awareness that you might not have had otherwise.

Simply pray that every person may find peace somewhere on their journey, in this life or the next.

117 Indignation

We can't meet self-righteous indignation with more of the same; it just leaves everyone feeling worse than when they started and shuts down any possibility of a solution.

While at times this may be hard to do, it is important to develop the willingness and discipline for it.

Rise above petty annoyances by challenging yourself in the face of these frustrations. Ask yourself, "What would be the most compassionate response possible in this situation?"

Be ready to apply the answer so that you might grow from the experience.

Resolve to shorten the time between knee-jerk reactions and more evolved responses in the face of situations that normally give rise to indignation.

Remember that you are striving for progress in this area, not perfection.

118 Discipline

When you think of the word *discipline,* do you think of it as punishment, a process, or a philosophy?

It technically means all of those things, but only the last two are necessary to reaching important goals.

If you're stuck on the first definition, you're not likely to get very far.

If you only concentrate on a process, disconnected from any core value, you'll enjoy some of the fruits of your labors, for sure, but you could get easily distracted from your goal if something more important arises.

If, however, your primary intent is on developing a particular expertise, embracing a school of thought, or claiming an area of specialty, then you are most likely to do the day-to-day, moment-by-moment tasks that will carry you to that goal.

In other words, if you are dedicated to the discipline of spirituality, then you will discipline yourself to meditate and pray each day.

119 Solutions

We can't force people to want solutions; we can only make them more inviting.

As a matter of fact, if you try to force answers on someone, they are quite likely to reject your every suggestion.

Leadership is the ability to start a new and productive conversation on an old problem, one that moves people to a fresh perspective and plan of action.

So smile.

Be encouraging.

Get excited about the possibilities.

Paint a picture of a better future.

Ask questions.

Stimulate others' ability to get creative.

Win them over.

120 Resolve

There are times when you run into one brick wall after another in pursuit of your goals and you feel like giving up on them, but you don't because somewhere inside of you is something telling you that you need to push on. You aren't sure you have the energy for it, but on the other hand you know you must . . . and on and on and on rages the internal dialogue in these circumstances.

You could always . . .

recommit,

eliminate the distractions that got you off the rail,

quiet your internal and external environment,

stop doing what you're doing, and do something else till the chaos passes,

step away and come back,

change your mind, the location, your view, your seat.

You can always start over.

121 Criticism

You know the scenario: Someone verbally slams someone else behind their back, leveling a judgment that annoys or angers you, or worse, has the potential to hook you into doing the same.

Your choices:

> Look at that person like his statement is the craziest thing you ever heard.

> Cock your head to one side and say, "Hmmm . . ."

> Get really mad and judge them back.

> Or, you could point out that their judgment doesn't seem like the most helpful thing to say by telling them:

> "I don't feel that judging that person that way is helpful."

> Then let go of any anger over the exchange, particularly if you've become frustrated that your response has had no positive effect on the conversation.

At the very least, take comfort in knowing that you don't engage in negative judging of others.

122 Enthusiasm

Get in touch with what inspires you, what makes you smile, what lightens your heart and lifts your spirit, and then share it enthusiastically.

You never know whom you'll motivate in the process.

123 A Prayer

Start the day in prayer, sincerely asking for direction on where and how you can best serve others with what you've been given.

Be completely open to the answers that are revealed.

Use this time to generate the focus, energy, and devotion that turn the day into a walking, talking, smiling meditation on how to make a positive mark in the world.

124 Rising Above

If you are able to rise above petty arguments, jealousy, gossip, and other forms of negativity, it doesn't mean you're a better person than everyone else; it simply means you're better at discerning what deserves your energy and attention and what doesn't.

Good for you.

Better still is the ability to teach others how to do the same, without displaying a shred of superiority in the process.

You set the example by how you leave those conversations—by being positive, hopeful, and forgiving as you exit.

This takes practice, like anything else, but once you commit to rising above negativity, and embody the above qualities as you do, maintaining your new nature is infinitely easier than engaging in things that foster resentment, anger, and fear.

125 Losing Resentments

We can't just wave a magic wand and make resentments about others disappear; it is not an intellectual decision.

We must have a spiritual process for making sense of the resentment. We must replace it with something more productive—like compassion—before we can let it go. Start by looking at whomever you believe is the cause of your unhappiness or resentment.

Imagine that this person's inability to do right by you has nothing whatsoever to do with you, that something else is standing in their way, something that may be causing them great unhappiness.

Generate understanding and compassion for them.

Pray for their happiness.

Pray some more.

Pray your way to sincerity.

Pray your way to forgiveness.

Keep praying until there is nothing left but a true desire for them to find peace and light.

And then you have let go.

Are you harboring any resentment against someone? Adopt this practice, and watch your resentment diminish as compassion and love grow.

126 Claim Your Greatness

Yes, you.

You, at your lightest, loveliest, most joyous, are who you are at your core.

It's also who you're meant to be out in the world.

See this.

Own it.

Be it.

Embrace and celebrate you—the ultimate you, the best you.

127 Reset

Fall in love with the idea that you can start your day over any time you need to, and be sure you also have a physical and emotional way to do so.

Simply stop what you're doing, stand up, take a big, deep breath, stretch your arms open wide, and gaze up at the sky as you lift your heart and give thanks.

This process should never fail to help you reset.

Sometimes all we need to do to get out of a funk is to physically and emotionally reset.

128 Self-Care

How we treat ourselves influences how we treat everyone and everything else; we cannot be any more kind, loving, patient, or compassionate with others than we are with ourselves.

Raise your standard of self-care—of mind, body, and soul—and the whole world benefits.

129 Freedom

As a spiritual being, you are free to step up to your gifts and talents, to answer your heart's calling.

You are surrounded by people who support you on this path.

You have the love of the Great Spirit.

It's time to grow, so affirm yourself by placing "I," "my," and "me" in the above statements. Say them out loud as often as necessary to keep you in a place of belief and focus.

130 Owning Your Part

Taking on someone else's part in an aggravating situation only delays owning and correcting your part.

Commit to shifting and improving how you come to the situation from here on, and resolve to let go of all anger and negative emotion associated with it.

Let everything else go, and put your attention on what you actually have the power to change, praying that everyone finds peace in the process.

Remember your boundaries; you cannot and should not fix everything. Know going in that you can do only what you can, and you're doing your best.

131 Clarity

The quickest way to clarity is through a calm mind.

Find your way to calm by seeing what is currently in the way of it.

Identify the obstacle, whether it is clutter, anxiety about something you know, or uncertainty about something you don't.

Now, sit quietly, eyes open, breathing easily.

Empty your mind.

Watch your thoughts.

Keep the ones that serve to bring you greater clarity, and let the others go.

Once your mind is filled with thoughts that serve the greater good, rise and meet the day.

132 Pushing On

Getting through difficult times means just that; that we keep pushing on and moving forward, that we don't let our challenges stop us.

Ask yourself, "Am I getting through my difficulties, or have I been stopped by them?"

If you're moving through, how are you able to do that despite the challenges? Who is helping you? What skills are you using? How are you being supported?

If you've been stopped, notice things about that too. What stopped you, and why? What needs to change in order to be on the move again? What else could change to provide an opening for progress?

An important part of pushing on and moving forward is being willing to examine things deeply in the time of resistance, not just after the fact.

133 Letting Go

To let go doesn't mean we no longer pay attention to something.

On the contrary, it means we know something better than ever, that we have made some distinction of thought that allows us to stop grappling and obsessing.

There is no true letting go without a lesson learned. To do otherwise is simply pretending something doesn't exist, as opposed to working with it for clarity and wisdom.

134 Acting "As If"

It's been said that the mind doesn't know the difference between what is real and what we imagine, so as long as we're thinking anyway we might as well be specific.

For instance, why not think, speak, and act—with clarity, confidence, and certainty—as if everything you ever wanted were already happening?

Why not see what that does to align the Universe with your vision?

Why not see who and what might show up as a result?

Daydreams don't have to be just fantasies; if you act as though things are the way you want them to be, they might just turn out that way in the end.

135 Action

Nothing cures anxiety better than action:

forward movement,

organization,

positive decisions (no matter how big or small),

enlisting others' help,

and giving thanks.

When you do these things, one at a time, in reference to something you're anxious about, you will notice very quickly how the action displaces your anxiety.

And when you complete one action, if anxiety arises again, pick another action to put in its place.

Don't wallow in anxiety; there is always something you can do to get unstuck.

136 Go for It

If you have a dream, one that could help countless people, what's stopping you from pursuing it?

Money? That doesn't have to stop you; there are plenty of success stories of people who made their dream come true off a cocktail napkin idea and the last of their savings.

Time? What better way is there to spend your time than in the service of others with your amazing gifts?

Uncertainty? Life is full of it, so you might as well experience the kind that comes with going for your goals and living your mission.

Maybe you hesitate because you look around, and nothing looks like it "goes" with your vision: You're not organized the way you think you should be, you don't have the materials you think you should, or you don't have the space to operate from.

More than anything, maybe you aren't certain how much of a risk to take to make your dream come true.

But every day you step out into the great unknown to get things done, one way or another, so why not do something that matters, that brings relief in some way to those who suffer? Better to do that than to play it safe and never make a mark.

Go for it; go full tilt in the direction of your dreams.

137 In Service

It's an amazing transformation, to go from being a taker to being a giver.

It is a transformation available to anyone who is willing to seek help, take the advice that is given, enjoy the fruits of those instructions and discipline, and pay that blessing forward by offering helpful advice and inspiration of their own.

That's how you get it done: by trying to take everything that comes your way and turn it into something useful for others.

You don't have to know exactly how you will be of service; simply start with the willingness to be, and see what unfolds.

138 Your Voice

We each have our own voice.

Some are casual, some formal. Some are high-pitched, some low. Some are fast, some are slow; some are loud, some are a whisper.

We tend to take our literal voice for granted—the tone, the pace, the inflection—and lose sight of whether it is speaking to our ideals and principles in a way that is most effective.

Don't be afraid to ask for feedback on your voice, whether it is your written or spoken words, to find out what people would like to hear more or less of.

Strengthen your literal and figurative voice by practicing articulation and enunciation; strive to make it rhythmic, clear, and engaging.

139 Daydreaming

Daydreaming is the ability to drift off and create a vision in your mind of the best people, places, and circumstances you can imagine.

It's most energizing when it is done for the sake of capturing a vision that you plan to put into action, as opposed to just doing it as an escape.

It's most effective when you give yourself a prescribed amount of focused time for it, where you really notice what scenarios grab your attention and compel you to manifest them.

Give yourself ten minutes to let your mind wander. See where it goes. Are there any things you've thought up that you can put into action in your real life?

140 Love

Don't hold back on love.

Definitely don't put it out there on the condition that you get love in return, or you're sure to be disappointed, because you can't control those results.

Instead, love for its own sake, an effort that never disappoints.

You are responsible for your own happiness, so decide to be loving, and love will come to you as a result.

It's lovely, this love thing.

141 Transforming Shame

Shame is by nature weighty, dark, and oppressive, a natural, human reaction to humiliation.

It is only appropriate to claim this emotion as a reaction to things we have done to others; we need not feel shame over that which has been done to us against our will.

Shame is also one of the most debilitating emotions to the human spirit if we fail to see it for what it is, and then resolve to learn and grow from what drove us to cause it.

To do that, we must face our shame, go toe to toe with it, tame it. Make it a critical part of our story instead of something to be banished, then make amends for it, and call it by a new and better name, like compassion, understanding, or humility.

As soon as we find the lesson in it, shame can become something positive and powerful, an actual vehicle by which we find healing for ourselves and others.

142 Hope

The beautiful thing about hope is that it's so easy to find; turn to it, and it is there.

Turn to hope figuratively: In your mind's eye, imagine yourself physically turning away from whatever source of negative energy might be causing you despair and toward the brilliant light of hope and possibility.

To literally turn to hope, find someone who has been through what you are going through, who gives you strength through his or her experience.

Connect with them, ask how they've done it, and thank them for their willingness to share.

143 Sacred Space

No matter how crazy things get, or how many things threaten to disrupt our environment—be it the landscape of our minds, our spirit, our bodies, or our external living space—we can make that space sacred by choosing to only let people and things into it that can significantly enhance it.

Start embracing the idea of "sacred space" by creating one in your home. It doesn't need to be big; it should just be clean, organized, and filled with items that represent calm, creativity, awareness, or whatever you want the space to stand for.

This is your sanctuary, that place where you can retreat, settle, and renew. Uphold the sanctity of this place, and you will find yourself more and more willing to claim sacred space in other areas of your life.

Do you have a sacred space? If no, create one. If yes, make time to maintain its sacredness.

144 Let It Out

We hold our breath for fear of what may overtake us.
We hold in our emotions for fear that they may overwhelm us.
We hold back on expressing our convictions for fear of
offending others.
We hold up our progress for fear of the unknown.
We hold out on love for fear of getting hurt.

Let it all out.
Breathe. Feel. Speak. Move. Love.

145 State of Mind

There are unique, physical ways to improve your emotional
state.

The power of words, for instance:

Happiness.

Joy.

Peace.

Prosperity.

Abundance.

Opportunity.

Say these words aloud one at a time, with feeling, and inflection, and volume.

Say them again, louder, with more feeling and inflection.

And again, louder still, with the biggest smile you can muster.

And again and again, until your emotional, physical, and mental state match the words.

Speak your way to happiness, peace, and abundance.

146 Love

Love is pretty handy, when you think about it.

It is bigger than anything we can imagine, and the smallest bit of it can make a world of difference.

It can cure what ails us, and soothe the savage beast of fear.

It picks us up, points us in the right direction, moves us along, cheers us on, and celebrates us.

It can dispel any negative emotion—greed, jealousy, envy, and the like—the moment we earnestly call on it to do so; the moment we invite it into our heart and soul and our every interaction.

What a wondrous and powerful force.

Remember the power and range of love today.

147 Talent

Everyone has a talent, some special ability to better someone else's life.

You have talent.

The only limitation to the power of your talent is in your mind, when you downplay its importance or hold back while you question whether it is "good enough" to share.

Any time you positively influence another to any degree through this talent is more than good enough; it is the ultimate expression of goodness.

You have a particular talent to bring to the world; by all means, bring it. Your gift is who you are in the process.

148 Freedom

If you want to be free of jealousy, contribute to someone else's success.

If you want to be free of greed, give till it hurts.

If you want to be free of resentment, work to better yourself.

If you want to be free of fear, cultivate your faith.

If you want to be free, surrender your ego.

What do you feel is tying you down? Find a way to make yourself free.

149 Pushing Back

No matter how put off you are by someone or something, you can learn to express your displeasure from a place of love and solution.

We're afraid that unless we ramp up our energy, and amp up the volume in the face of what irks us, we will be walked on, taken advantage of, or prevented from speaking our truth.

The truth is, if you maintain your overall love of humanity during difficult times, you will be more able to say how you feel and take a stand as needed, without losing your temper or your personal power.

Discipline yourself to think before you speak, pause before you act, weigh the facts before you judge, and you are likely to find the most appropriate response to any negative situation.

It's easy to be calm, cool, and collected when things are going right. Imagine how effective it is to be that way in response to what might normally rattle your cage door off its hinges.

It may not be the most popular response, but it will likely be the most helpful one.

150 Inspiration

If you want to lead a new and inspiring conversation, you can't keep indulging in the old ones, the fearful ones, the small and questioning ones.

There is someone in your life, right now, who needs your inspiration, who is ready to see you in a more positive light, who has already let go of who you were in the past and is just waiting for the moment when you are ready to do the same.

And the great news is, you don't have to worry about being original; just wonder how to be more motivational, more positive, and more encouraging.

Inspiration starts with you.
And maybe you're the one who needs your inspiration most.

151 The Journey

Sometimes you find yourself putting one foot in front of the other, trudging along, but with no clear vision of where you're going, or what you'll do once you get there. It's easy to lose sight of our goals, to get lost on the path, or disconnected from what set us out to begin with.

Just stop, take a breather, and regroup about what you're after and why. Once you figure it out, if you're on the right path to that goal already and just needed to look up through the trees for a bit to see the sun, then hopefully you're now feeling refreshed, and ready to resume the journey.

If you find you need to alter your path, don't despair; better that you discover it now than get any further down the same road.

152 Appreciation

We are most likely to find additional opportunities in life when we cultivate a great appreciation for exactly where we are today, and with whom, with what we already have.

Finding and embracing gratitude for today doesn't mean we stop striving; we bring it all with us, all the gratitude we can muster for whatever we've learned up till now that keeps us moving in a positive direction.

And if all that striving is in service to others as well as you, you can't go wrong.

Appreciate the gifts you have in your life today; they are what will deliver you to future gifts down the road.

153 Supporting Your Mission

We do so much, run in so many different directions.

We are called upon by so many people, for so many different reasons.

Without a unifying thread of mission to bind these activities, it can all end up feeling like oh so much to do, without much of a sense of purpose—much less accomplishment—at the end of the day.

Establish your mission in all categories of your life and it will become clear what needs to be done each day, what you will need to say yes to, and what you need to say no to.

It might not be easy at first to shift your yeses and nos to support your mission, but it will give you a sense of focus, direction, and cohesive thought like no other.

154 Authenticity

Being authentic means that you're not trying so hard to be you:

> You say the thing that bubbles up if you believe it can be helpful, and hold your tongue if it can't;

> Maybe you soften the edges of your thoughts if it will help you get your message across, but you are no less sure of your opinions if you do;

> You say what's true for you without worrying about whether others agree;

> You don't make others wrong for having opinions or lifestyles contrary to yours;

> You can be counted on;

> You don't embellish for dramatic effect, just to be noticed;

> What you see is what you get;

> You are genuinely happy with who you are, and it shows.

How can you live more authentically?

155 Forgiveness

Give people room to be better than you thought they were.

Give them credit for their efforts.

Stop comparing them to an old version you have of them in your mind.

Stop competing with their moments of goodness.

Give them love.

You've been wanting them to change, but if you've decided that change must be at a certain pace to be "good enough" for you to forgive them for their past transgressions, then that isn't really forgiveness, just controlled judgment.

Give others the benefit of the doubt. You'd appreciate the same kindness in return.

156 Motivation

We're not really motivated by the things we think we are.

We hear people say they are motivated by money, for instance, but what that usually means is that they are motivated by the freedom or security or sense of power they think money brings.

It's not things we're after; nice things are nice, but they're no guarantee of happiness, after all.

It's a feeling, a vision; a meaningful sense of ourselves in relation to the world that really drives us in a sustainable way.

If you're looking to be freshly inspired, then look inside, reconnect with your values, and find and engage with external elements—the people, places, and things—that support and encourage them.

157 Pleasure

If you are about love, then it brings you great pleasure to give love, to receive love, and to witness love.
If you are about kindness, then it is deeply satisfying to be kind and to know kindness.
If you are about spirituality, then you are delighted to be filled with the spirit of your higher power, and to share that with others.

True pleasure, then—as in deep, abiding joy—comes from manifesting and witnessing our principles in action.
Where will you find your joy today?

158 Power

There are great exchanges of power going on all the time.

There is the power we give others, and that which we afford ourselves.

There is temporary power, and there is permanent power.

There is power that is instantly bestowed based on someone's role, and power that is earned regardless of position.

There is power on earth, and power from above.

Be mindful to what or whom you give power; in doing so, you give permission to influence your behavior or alter your path, for better or for worse.

159 Being Practical

You can be a dreamer and be organized at the same time.

You can be wildly imaginative, and wonderfully practical.

You can be beautifully poetic, and still be sensible.

As a matter of fact, one of the best things you can do to support your wild and wonderful imagination, to have the energy you need to go after your dreams, is to make sure the practical demands—the schedules, systems, and accountability—that support them are cared for.

160 People

Be fascinated by people in terms of what makes them tick, what drives them, what they love and what they don't, and why.

When you are fascinated, you are curious, and willing to see people from different angles and learn about what moves them.

And when you're willing to see more sides of others, and to learn what they value, you will see aspects of them that remind you of yourself—the good, the great, and the not-so-much—which will remind you of our common humanity.

You see them, and you see you.
Learn from them, and you will learn more about you.

161 Conscious Awareness

We learn differently as adults.

The good news is that when we're grown up, we have way more choice in what we learn; we can choose subjects that align with our daily lives and support our values.

The challenging news is that we often confuse an intellectual understanding of something with actual learning, which is the full assimilation of information into our daily habits.

Before we can know whether to fully adapt our lessons, we have to take a leap of faith and try them out a bit, see what happens, notice the shifts, try again, try yet again from a different angle, and learn some more.

And once we've done that—the trying and the noticing and the trying again—we will see whether to take the lesson on full bore.

It's one thing to be taught; it's quite another to learn whether or not to integrate the teaching.

162 Self-Obsession

It takes an act of God for some people to see that not everything revolves around them.

Not a metaphoric act; a real act of God, whatever God is.

It usually takes a wholesale spiritual and psychic change—under great duress—to stop taking everything in life so personally.

So when things bother you, consider whether you're taking things too personally.

Then pray to be released from the bondage of self-centeredness (over and over until it sticks).

Try giving the suffering that comes from selfishness over to some power greater than yourself.

163 Teamwork

Teamwork starts with how you greet the day.

If you start with a spirit of collaboration, you will open innumerable doors, create surprising partnerships, and reveal unforeseen opportunities.

If you do so not only for your own good, but for others as well, you will multiply those opportunities immeasurably.

There is so much good we can do for so many when we aim to do it together.

164 False Pride

There comes a time when it is critical—lifesaving, actually—to lay out all your fears and insecurities.

It lets people really see you, all sides of you, with all your worries and confidences, the ups and the downs, the good thoughts and the bad.

It also helps you settle into the groove that is you: not what you do or who you serve, but who you are, because letting people in this way turns on your authentic light.

If you are always matter-of-fact about the hard parts of your life, others will assume that everything is always OK, and you will miss many opportunities to get the help you need.

If you share your pain in the spirit of letting someone know where you really are in that moment, the moment can bring you answers.

165 Consistency

If you are consistent, a day at a time, with some action forward, there's no doubt you'll get somewhere.

The question is, are today's consistencies leading you to a favorable tomorrow?

You have to match your habits of today with your dreams of tomorrow if you're to stand a chance of making those dreams come true.

It's easy to drift off course, to let certain things creep into your daily life that work against your dreams. You might be working out, for instance, but slowly, without thinking about it, you're eating too much ice cream every night before bed.

Awareness takes consistency, too—a consistent effort to review the day's activities, and to map out the ones to come, to see that they are still aligned with what matters to you most.

166 Ambition

If you only have your ultimate goals in mind, and no time or patience for all the stops and starts it takes to reach them, then you're likely to miss some wondrous opportunities to develop all kinds of different skills and perspectives along the way.

Don't forget, there is no destination without a journey.

And it really isn't some arduous trip to be "put up" with, but a rather remarkable one when we embrace the whole of it as necessary and right and valuable.

Whether we get to our end goal or not, if we keep our eyes open we'll get something very valuable out of the journey in every case.

167 Rebirth

To be given the opportunity to rise above shame and humiliation, to be forgiven for our transgressions and invited into
the light of a promising new life can sometimes feel like
more than we deserve.

But why deny yourself the opportunity when it presents
itself?

It's no good to play the martyr and hold yourself out
to the world as one who has just done wrong and never
deserves better.

It's far better to show people what's possible when you
face your past, make up for your misdeeds, and accept the
grace of a new future.

**You deserve a great life if you're willing to accept it, be
humbled by it, and use it for the greater good.**

168 First Light

First look at what the morning calls you to see and
appreciate.

Sit wherever you have the most comfortable seat and the
most engaging view, be it of something inside and near you,
or just outside the window.

Soften your eyes, soften your breathing, and just drink in the visual before you, taking time to appreciate every nuance of what's in front of you, every sight and smell and shape and sound.

The rest of the day will certainly have its turn.

Bring the awareness you have upon awakening to the whole day. See the world with fresh eyes.

169 Conviction

Will you only speak of peace and love to those who would agree, or will you stand up for these principles in the face of those who would vehemently oppose them?

Standing up for peace and love doesn't mean fighting to make a point. It means resolving, more than ever, to embody them and advocate for them.

The more angry and hateful someone gets, the more peaceful and loving we must try to be. The moment we take on their anger, their hate, their opposition to right thinking, is the moment we have given in to lesser principles.

We all have people who test us. How best can you stand up for peace and love in response to another's lack of it?

170 Gratitude Exercise

You already know why it's so important to give thanks for the emotional, mental, physical, spiritual, and financial benefits you enjoy: It keeps you humble, and hopefully it keeps you from taking those things for granted.

You also know how to identify your present-day blessings and express thanks for them in word and deed; you probably have scores of exercises for doing so.

Here's one more, just in case you need a new way to generate gratitude: Go back in your mind and choose an event from your life that seems unexceptional. Then look to where it led—whom you met as a result, what you learned, and how it changed you for the better.

Do this any time you need to be reminded of how the most ordinary events can lead to some of the most important moments of growth.

171 Stubbornness

If you're fighting to be the one with all the answers, then it's time to loosen your grasp (maybe literally as well as figuratively), on being the all-knowing source.

Always look to be helpful; don't worry so much about being in charge.

Give other people and possibilities a chance to contribute and present; be more cooperative than competitive.

Let go; stay involved.

172 Vanity

You can spend a lifetime pursuing the adoration of those who know little about you,
or you can spend this moment with those who know you best;
those who "get" you, who give you a sense that you've lived lifetimes together, lifetimes ago;
those with whom you have the most precious of connections.
It is far better to be truly seen than to be merely recognized.

Today, be with the closest people in your life. Settle in with them, and let no one else be more important than they are.

173 Love

Love is not hard, except when we layer it with expectations of how it will be received or reciprocated.

On its own, there is nothing easier or more pure than love.

Be loving today, for its own sake; let love fill you up and spill out of you, and have absolute faith that it will touch someone on some level, and that you don't have to know how for that to be true.

174 Usefulness

What is the one thing you need to do today to be of best use to all?

It may not be as esoteric a thing as you may think—it might be that being organized is what's best, or conscientious, or attentive, or calm.

It's probably a combination of all these things and more, but pick the one that seems to be what's needed most of all, and focus there.

We're always making an effort; the question is whether it's a conscious one.

175 Pivotal Moments

Our lives can turn on a dime.

With one fell swoop, everything we know can change.

Sometimes it's a tragedy that turns us, sometimes it is life's comedy; sometimes the world is turned for us, sometimes we turn the world.

Sometimes we learn from change quickly, sometimes slowly.

The blessings of these turnings will always materialize, if we look for them.

176 Gentle Thinking

Don't force your thoughts; rather, give them time and room to arise, to reveal themselves while you patiently observe them and decide which are worth following.
We are so used to thinking and doing, thinking and doing.

It's a nice change of pace to simply sit for a time, with one subject or another, notice what comes up, and then carefully choose your actions.

The same is true with speech:

We don't always have to fill space with words.
Sometimes we can let stillness and silence rule.

177 Now

We have this amazing freedom that comes with being awake and alive, and of a clear and sound mind, all this energy that enables us to stir up all kinds of excitement in our life.

In the flurry we create, we must remember not to get so wrapped up in what's ahead for us that we miss the beauty of this moment, right here, the one we're sitting with right now.

178 Expectations

Don't be upset or surprised when people don't live up to expectations you've never expressed to them.

How is someone supposed to know you want things a certain way if you never told them?

It may seem easier to make someone bad or wrong than to take responsibility for not clarifying your wishes in the first place. It's not.

179 Grief

Grief comes in waves. Some you see coming, most you don't.

And the waves bring great uncertainty: Where have our loved ones gone? What are they doing now?

And with that uncertainty comes more sorrow, for the lack of answers to these very important questions.

But it's OK. The waves, the uncertainty, the lack of answers needn't knock us down and take us under.

The stronger we learn to stand in those waters, the less power they will have to overtake us.

We learn to stand strong by turning our sadness into a celebration of the impact and legacy of the people we've lost.

180 Inspiration Overload

We are inundated with so many messages meant to move and inspire us—words and pictures and videos, from our tablets and computers and phones and readers and blogs and websites and email and social media and tweets—so much so that it all starts to run together and lose its power . . .

. . . maybe leaving us a little breathless from the sheer volume of it,

which isn't the main intent of all these well wishes, I'm sure.

We're in danger of losing our ability to be truly moved because we are spending so little time with so much information, rather than truly studying, contemplating, and taking action with fewer messages for greater impact.

So step back and ask yourself which sources of inspiration speak to you. Commit to following that advice for a period, letting all the extra "guru speak" go for the time being, so that the messages can regain power for you.

181 Your Story, Your Gift

Nothing has greater influence on any aspect of your life than your story, or what you tell yourself is right, true, or possible.

Personally, professionally, emotionally, mentally, spiritually, physically, or financially, this story informs every move you make.

And it doesn't matter where the story started—except perhaps as a point of reference for how far you've come. What matters is what that story is now, and that it is written to serve your greatest good in all the categories of life.

Pick one category of your life.

Write a statement in reference to it that starts with "I am . . ." Tell how you'd like to be in this area, as though it's already true.

Next, choose three actions you will take to align your external environment with this new internal truth.

Schedule these actions, complete them, and celebrate them every step of the way.

Before you know it, your external and internal realities will tell the same powerful story.

Take every opportunity you can to serve others with your story.

182 Expertise

If you are constantly improving, tweaking, trying on, and experimenting with new ways of thinking, acting, and being, personally or professionally, will you ever establish your expertise in any arena?

To settle into a version of yourself that people can easily identify doesn't necessarily mean you've compromised your talents, or accepted a smaller version of your ultimate potential—it hopefully means you've cleared up any remaining confusion in your mind of exactly what you stand for and have to offer.

There is grace in simplicity. Know your talents, and develop them into something great.

183 Precious Human Birth

With this precious human existence, we have the extraordinary opportunity to not just meet but also deeply engage with brilliant, creative, and loving souls around the world.

We expand our capacity to receive the infinite blessings of this world . . .

> by getting on the path of self-examination and improvement;
>
> by becoming people of impact and spirit and hope;
>
> by returning to and embracing the love with which we came into the world; and
>
> by appreciating the choice that was made—however that came to be—for us to appear here, in this time, in this form, with this amazing opportunity to make a real difference.

How will you take advantage of your precious life today?

184 Sacred Space

A deep and unshakable connection is formed when you create a sacred space dedicated to your innate wisdom and creativity.

You create that sacred space the moment you wholeheartedly agree to.
And in that space, you will connect with the Divine.

185 To Retreat

As much as we love to engage, there is also a time and place for full retreat, to silence and settle our bodies, minds, and spirits, and regain the strength so necessary to furthering our missions in life.

It may be the biggest action you can take in support of your dreams today.

Make time to retreat; find the place, then breathe, relax, reflect, wonder, and drift.

186 Critics

Putting yourself or your work out for review causes some people great anxiety; we can be very sensitive to criticism.

However, feedback is critical to gauging our impact, so these reviews can provide an extraordinary chance to hone our skills.

In order to push through the fear of review, choose a different word or perspective for the experience. For instance, you can see your chosen audience as a "focus group," rather than "critics."

Simple semantics just may help in keeping you more open to receiving others' feedback, and you might have room to improve from their comments.

187 Amends

Many personal development programs teach the process of amends, to right one's wrongs not only by apology, but also with an offering of how to make things better.

You must also learn to say when you are hurt by someone's actions, and let go of whether you receive an amends in return.

Let your stand be its own reward.
It's more like speaking your piece than searching for an apology.

188 To Teach

What a privilege it is
to kindle the wisdom of others,
as a parent, teacher, or closed-mouth friend.

May we speak with humility,
listen with compassion,
and find genuine joy in the exchange.

189 Intentions

Let's do love today.

Let's do kindness and wonder and joy.

Let's do gratitude, spirit, forgiveness, and compassion.

Let's do life, lightly.

Intend for the best.

190 Staying the Course

Your convictions are your own to manage; no one else is responsible for whether you follow whatever course you've chosen.

Be grateful for fellow travelers—thank goodness you don't have to go it alone—but don't make your progress contingent on their willingness to walk the same path, the same way, at the same pace, or you're bound to second-guess every step and never really advance.

Be confident in your path, and support others in their chosen path as well.

191 Conscientious Objection

In our social, religious, moral, and political landscapes, there is much on which to disagree, and great potential for mudslinging, gloating, and hostile exchange as each person campaigns for their side.

Such conduct does nothing ultimately to support a cause, and indeed may sway people in the opposite direction by its very hostility.

Better that we find a way to fight for our beliefs without compromising our sense of human decency in the process.

May we claim our principles without condemning others
who don't share them;
may we discern what is right for us without making others
wrong;
may we take a stand with grace, dignity, and respectful
certainty.

192 Cooperation

Sometimes we work very hard to cultivate the false illusion
that we are neither a follower nor a joiner, that we are fiercely
independent and don't need a bunch of other people getting
in the way of our progress.

The truth is, we may simply need more practice on how
to be with people in a meaningful way, whether by leading a
charge or carrying out someone else's directives.

It takes so much work to cultivate the illusion that we
can do this life thing all on our own, so much energy to get
people to hear our fierce battle cries of independence. Is it
worth the trouble to earn this "badge of honor"?

How much easier it is—and more invigorating—to honor
our interdependence, to fully engage with our shared
need for knowledge, encouragement, and love.

193 The Ultimate Awakening

If there is one virtue above all others to awaken to, it is the realization that our suffering is caused by attachment and aversion, by our obsessive drive to achieve more happiness and to avoid more suffering.

To release ourselves from obsessing over the pursuit of happiness and avoidance of suffering, and the pain that comes with them, perhaps we simply need to agree that the only thing that matters is our service to others, and have faith that the results are up to a power much greater than ourselves.
     Perhaps.

194 Visions

Pay attention to the visions that call to you when you're awake or asleep.
     You don't have to chase them, react to them, worry or obsess over them.
     Just walk with them, mindfully, so that if they continue to summon you, you can meet them and respond to them with clarity and wisdom.

Today, face things head-on. Your intuition is always trying to tell you things if you're open to listening.

195 Progress

Be fascinated by who you've become just since yesterday because of the experiences, epiphanies, people, and spiritual shifts you've encountered.

Be mindful of which of these you've carried into today.

Be curious about which of them you will carry into tomorrow.

Be conscious of who you might become as a result.

Progress doesn't happen overnight. Appreciate the steps you've taken along the way, and the steps you will take in the future, to accomplish your goals.

196 Inventory

Not enough can be said about the power of the conscious act of a searching, fearless, and thorough evaluation of our conduct, past and present.

Sure, it can be scary to look at our behavior and its consequences, but it is worse to sit with the fear of what may happen if we don't.

And inventory isn't just to assess the negative events of our lives; it is also quite useful to look at what's gone very, very right, and own our part in that as well.

The blessings that can come from looking into the events of our lives and coming away with a road map for change are endless.

197 Deserving

No one taps us on the head at birth and decides whether or not we are worthy of a happy life.

Some experience happiness in spite of their upbringing, some because of it, so history is not an absolute harbinger of the future, good or bad.

The beautiful news is that if you're not where you want to be now in life, you have a shot at improving it the moment you decide you are worthy of grace and opportunity.

Others already believe that about you.

It's your turn to believe, to invite grace and opportunity into your life, and be available to its direction.

198 Do the Right Thing

Put your faith not in what will come to be by managing your mind for the greater good, but in who you will become.

You won't gain control of the future through conscious conduct, but you will greatly influence it by your behavior.

It's the right thing to do, to right ourselves, right our past, right our sense of virtue and morality, to come to life with the right intentions.

Where can you do right today?

199 Small Things, Big Stories

Take a pen and paper, and sit somewhere in your house that you don't normally.

Close your eyes, and settle your body and mind with a few deep breaths.

Open your eyes, and write for five minutes about the first thing you see and the first thought about what you see.

Keep writing, finding perspective and description and story in what you see.

When the five minutes are up, read what you've written. Notice what you've learned from what you saw and wrote about.

There is beauty in the mundane, if we're only willing to slow down enough to notice it.

200 Winning the Battle

Half the battle of life is to see life as something other than a battle.
Life can be hard.
It isn't always hard.
Whether it is or it isn't oftentimes depends on how you look at it.

The trick is to not let the hard times form your global perspective on life.

201 Prayer

What could be more awesome than the power of prayer, how it calms your body, focuses your mind, lifts your spirits, and puts marvelous things in motion by its very intention.

No matter what or whom you pray to, the very act of plugging into a power greater than yourself can be enough to stimulate a complete rebirth of hope, love, compassion, and forgiveness.

It's as simple as asking for the above ideals to be present for all and being willing to be a vessel of those blessings as best you can on this given day.

There may be no greater instrument for change.

Practice the power of prayer today.

202 Surrender

How powerful our egos must be, to deny us, for even one second, the freedom that comes from surrender:

surrender to love,

surrender to spirit;

surrender to ultimate wisdom.

As strong as that ego may be, a small cry of "I give," with a smile on, hands up, and your heart open, might be all that's needed to stop struggling and let love, spirit, and wisdom reign anew.

203 Rejection

It doesn't seem to matter how old we get, we still worry about whether or not people will like us and want to engage with us.

To step out of our comfort zone and invite people in, knowing full well that they may reject us, is a big leap indeed.

But invite we must, for who are we without others with whom to reflect, encourage, and suppose?

Keep inviting others to come out and play; after all, that's how the best of friends are made.

204 Pain

It's next to impossible to make sense of our pain when we're in the middle of it.

We must step back from it, take a longer view of it, maybe turn away from it altogether—if even for a moment—to take a breath and reconnect with our primary purpose in whatever area of life we are struggling.

When we take determined action in the face of our confusion, rather than giving in to our base reactions, we can better see if what's torturing us merits any more of our time and energy, and if so, now meet it with a peaceful resolve to find sustainable relief.

205 Resentment

There isn't a single good reason to hold on to resentment.

It doesn't make a hurtful situation any less so.

On the contrary, it only brings more hurt, which causes more resentment—on and on, deepening our wounds until they threaten to permanently scar us.

Deal with the initial pain: Understand it, resolve it, find compassion and forgiveness for it; work with all manners of healing from it.

And then let it go.

206 Meditation

Quieting the mind and the body creates the most magical space in which to connect with our intuition, our "sense" of things.

As you sit, if you sense anxiety, you can breathe it away.

If you sense anger or fear, you can lean into it and work with it—find faults with its construction—or lean away and let it go.

If you are agitated, you can find calm; if you are sluggish, you can reenergize.

If you sit and open the space between your thoughts, you will know how best to serve this day.
You'll just know.

207 Look Up

Look up—there it is, a whole new life, with new perspectives and possibilities, new friends and ideas; a new freedom and happiness.

Look up, and find a new way to participate in life, with your mind on more than you and your needs.

Look up, and find spirit, love, hope, and guidance.
Look up, and find God.
Look up.

208 Pay Attention

Give the gift of your full attention, with your mind, your eyes, your smile, your stance; it may be all someone needs to reconnect with their own sense of worth and purpose.

That goes for you, too.

Turn your mind toward the vision of your highest potential. See it in all its glory; smile to recognize its radiance; let it lift you, heart, soul, and body to your highest height; and know that you are meant for greatness in all things.

If you can't envision your highest potential right now, recognize that without judging yourself too harshly, and commit to finding the right time to do so.

209 Special Moments

Life brings these exquisite wrap-you-up-and-don't-let-go-just-yet moments where you hold still and simply enjoy the time to appreciate connection and love.

Find those special moments today.
Better yet, create them.
In any event, cherish them.

210 Teach

It is one thing to teach; it's quite another to argue or sell a point.

Do you want me to consider a point of view and come to my own conclusion, or are you intent on seeing that I come to yours?

Are you trying to move and inspire me, or persuade and "win" me?

If you want to teach me, first learn how I learn (through pictures, words, or tales), know what I know and am attached to (my values, goals, and experiences), and then ask me to contemplate a new perspective.

When you're teaching, teach with care. Knowing your audience and your desired outcome before deciding which approach to use makes all the difference in the end.

211 Accepting Grace

Perhaps the only real struggle in this life is the shift of allowing our minds, bodies, and souls to accept the grace and opportunity that surround and await us.

This is a huge shift, made only more difficult by letting trivial things get in the way of it.

Learn to recognize and honor what is truly important to you, and you will be less inclined to let yourself get bogged down by the people, places, and things that stand in your way.

212 Generosity

Sometimes people are just generous, without solicitation.
There's no need to question why.
They just are.

Generosity is a two-way street; just sincerely say thank you as you either accept or decline a gift.

213 Suspending Judgment

For a moment, put aside your negative judgments about the difficult relationships in your life—the things you've decided about them from afar—and resolve instead to understand them, to learn everything you can about who these people are and what they value, so you can make decisions based on whole knowledge rather than a collection of emotions and assumptions.

Don't just write someone off because you're uncomfortable getting to know him or her.

Learn how to interact, to engage, to foster better and better communication, for their sake and yours, for now and for the future.

By suspending judgment, many of your frustrations can be lifted as you cease to write people off or carry lingering resentments toward them.

214 Your Voice

Don't worry about finding your voice. Do what you're called to, what will best serve others, and your voice will find you.
Don't let your concern over finding the "right" words keep you from saying anything at all.
Don't let your fear that others will disagree keep you from taking a stand.

Don't put off till tomorrow what you could joyously express today.

215 Clear Your Mind

Clear away the fear, anger, resentment, and other negative habits of mind that cloud the brilliant light of your intuition.

Breathe, dance, write, sing, meditate, and pray them away so the world can once again be warmed by your wisdom.

216 Making It Easy

We say (OK, sometimes we insist) that certain situations or tasks, while simple, are not easy. But perhaps that's only because we've never practiced making them so.

What if we learned to ease into the situation?

What if we brought a settled mind and an easy nature to the task?

What if we used a gentle, easy hand in responding to what agitates us?

Certain circumstances might never be a total breeze, but remembering to take it easy in all things can eventually make them so much easier to get through.

217 Standards

Most of the time, we respond to life with long-established values.

But sometimes we are forced to completely rethink those values by issues which test all of our standards, devotion, and resolve, forcing us to ask ourselves, "What am I most committed to here?"

There's no need to feel pressured to instantly switch positions; instead, take a careful look at what you feel compelled to do, what principles you are drawn to and certain of because of the greater effect they will have on your life and others'.

Today could be the day you take a whole new stand for your life.
Or it could be the day that you make a deeper commitment to your current stance.
Either way, this reflection could make for a pretty exciting day.

218 Impressions

Let's strive to manage our conduct so well that if our most recent impression on someone becomes our last, it is a favorable one.

Be positive, gracious, and joyful whether you're meeting someone for the first time, or the hundredth. Our actions have more of an impact than we can know.

219 Grow in Usefulness

Strive to become an expert at something beneficial to humankind—humor, love, kindness, and the like—and your days will be more fulfilling than you can imagine.

Certainly you're an expert at one of these (or something similar) already.
If not, it's a lot of fun to practice becoming one.

220 Many Paths

Our lives are the result of following a crazy beautiful collection of suggestions and steps from many worlds; perhaps we should defend till the end a person's right to choose which path works best for their journey.

We aim for recovery from what ails us, for spiritual awakening, and a chance to be contributing members of society.

That we get there is the goal; how we do so is each person's choice.

Yes, we have our biases for the best process for redemption, based on our experience; however, it does no good to condemn someone's decision to get there by a different route.

221 To Love

Thinking of love, be mindful that it is an action we take, not a feeling we seek.

Joy is its byproduct.
To love is to find joy.

The only pain that comes with love is our attachment to it; on its own, there is nothing more pure or rewarding.

222 Lighten Up

Today's topic for discussion is what it means to "lighten up."

It means to take oneself less seriously.

Seriously, that's it.

Because the less serious you are, the less perturbed you will be by others.

If you're all light and playful and unburdened and stuff, chances are you'll be rising way above the petty stuff (yours or others').
Seriously, try it.

223 Effective vs. Busy

We're so, so, so busy.

It's really quite an accomplishment these days to do what we really want or feel we need to with never enough time.

So if we're not doing what we want to or need to, what exactly are we up to? And how did we get there?

Maybe it's time to look at all the things we've said yes to that have us running around with no time and evaluate whether some of them could stand to be said no to.

At least one or two of them, anyway.

And there's no need to rush to fill the blanks of time that we free by adjusting our yeses and nos.

Don't just pray for more time. Ask to be graced with wisdom, clarity, and inspiration, then choose the tasks, service, and circumstances that are most likely to provide them.

224 Emotionally Present

Instead of denying your feelings, stay with the exact perspective or emotion that you're feeling at the moment and work with it. See it for what it is; examine it for its merits, or lack thereof; and then decide what to do next.

Journaling is a particularly effective way to work through negative emotions (and by negative, I certainly don't mean "bad").

Write about exactly what you're feeling, and just keep writing until it starts to take a shape that you're satisfied with.

You may not come out of the despair or grief immediately, but it may not yet be the point to do so, anyway.

What you will get is an opportunity to see, right in front of you, in your own words, what's going on for you and what you want to do with it.

Happy or sad, it works both ways.

In opening ourselves to our emotions, we can work through them more quickly or appreciate their gift more fully, depending on the circumstance. Whatever you're feeling, feel it deeply.

225 Imagine

Imagine that you know exactly how you want to be of best service in the world,

that you see everything you need to see,

that you have everything you need;

that you are exactly who you need to be to fulfill your mission.

All that's left is cultivating the willingness to step up to that vision.

Think about why you want to be of maximum service, why it's a "must" for you to live from a deep sense of purpose. Let your "why" be your guiding force—the how, when, where, and with whom will reveal itself in time.

226 Moving Through Pain

It is possible to benefit by moving slowly through pain, by not attacking it and causing more agitation, or rushing through it and losing the lesson on how to prevent it in the future.

Today, try to meet your pain where it is.
Breathe there and loosen everything that surrounds it.

Then move in deeper, breathe more, dissolve more,
move deeper still,
noticing what caused and sustains the pain and breathing
through that,
until you move all the way through it and can rest.

227 Hope and Fear

It is fascinating to examine what drives us to grow in
love and usefulness and what prevents us, to look at what
increases our hope and decreases our fear.

First we must get to a point where being loving and
useful is our biggest priority. That usually happens when we
finally tire of exhausting everyone (ourselves included) with
the weight of our self-centeredness.

Once we turn our attention more fully to the service
of others, we can find almost instant relief, the kind that
will likely motivate us to continue until service becomes the
reigning principle in our lives.

Making that shift won't eliminate your fears; you'll just
find less time for them once you're more focused on service.

So define and engage with what matters; avoid or eliminate what doesn't.

Spend more time cultivating hope, less time indulging
fear.

Do it through journals, prayer, meditation, reading, more writing, talking, scheduling, doing, analyzing, tracking, and duplicating what works.

Shift your focus outward, to the service of others, with all your might, and you will wake to find you've made more of an impact than you ever knew you could.

228 Progress

Progress is seeing life as a series of things that happen in the world, rather than a series of things that happen to you.

Remember the world is not about you; it is about us all.

229 Open to Suggestion

Imagine just how far we'd all get—and how fast—if our egos didn't insist on having the last (or the first) word on our solutions.

Imagine the magnitude and velocity of our growth if we were all just completely open to information and support, no matter the source.

Imagine.

230 Be Brilliant

The time is exactly right for some piece of your brilliance to manifest.

Don't hold back, waiting for the other bits to catch up;

give this one the spotlight, the stage, the audience,

for the sake of whom you might move by your performance.

Don't be afraid to shine.

231 Claim Your Talents

Skip the laziness of self-deprecation, and go straight to a humble articulation of where you excel, and the impact you have on others as a result.

We need your gifts,

your leadership,

your enthusiasm and certainty.

We need you to own your brilliance, so we might better embrace our own.

232 Grief

Do not let the heavy stones of grief weigh you down, steal your breath, and render you useless.

Instead, with your pain build a platform on which to stand, celebrate life, and comfort others in their time of pain.

Do not let grief crush you.

233 Fight or Flight?

That depends on the battle, and whether you'd be fighting (or fleeing) for the right reasons.
That depends on whether you're just trying to avoid pain and find pleasure.

Dig in and change, or leave and hope for better?
That depends on where the most beneficial change is more likely to occur.

In the midst of any momentous decision or painful struggle, flight is often our first instinct.

We have a great desire for certainty, which doesn't make us bad people, just nervous humans sometimes.

But if we don't take time to analyze what's triggering our fight-or-flight response, we're in danger of making a move, any move, as long as it brings the illusion of assurance.

So sit (unless it puts you in danger to sit—you wouldn't stand your ground if a literal pack of lions were coming at you). Sitting gives you time to objectively look at the situation, consult with your trusted advisors, and then make a thoughtful decision.

When faced with a tough decision, start by praying to be led to where you will learn the deepest lessons that will help the greatest number of people, and resist the urge to go where you will be the most comfortable the soonest.

234 Asking for Help

There's a big difference between telling people about our problems and actually asking for help.

The former is self-seeking, and indulgent; the latter is productive, as it seeks a solution.

The next time you find yourself caught up in pain and confusion, rather than obsessing over "What's wrong with me?" look at whether you've yet stopped to ask for direction. Have you engaged others for their perspective? Or have you been intent on going it alone?

If you find that your own best advice isn't improving things, it's probably way past time to enlist some help.

In the future, the more you train yourself to accept direction, the more you'll find yourself thinking "problem solved," rather than "crisis averted."

235 Learning Greatness

We can't just think our way to greatness; we must develop real skills for such, in thought, language, and deed.

Practice changing your mind,

speaking your truth,

doing things outside your comfort zone in support of your goals, your mission.

Honor your "musts."

236 Love and Joy

Let's do love today.
Let's do love, hope, humor, spirit, and joy.

In no particular order.
For no particular reason.
Perhaps all at once.

Make this day wonderful by bringing love to the world.

237 The Path to Certainty

Sometimes we're just not sure what to do next.

We get scattered, disorganized, feel tentative—even a little afraid.

Until you remember your one guiding mission, whatever that may be.

Let's pretend that your mission is to better yourself for the sake of whom you might serve.

The question then becomes, "What do I need to do (physically, emotionally, mentally, spiritually, financially) to have the greatest impact?

Pen to paper, map out your impact plan, and schedule the action items into your day, secure in the knowledge that while you won't get it all perfectly right every time, you will have chosen the perfect intention with which to move through the day.

238 Be Careful

Today might be a day to be quiet and careful.

Not wary, but methodical.

Literally take things one at a time, allowing the next thing and the next and the next into your consciousness as they arise in the calendar, instead of constantly searching for what to think and say and do now or next.

Today might be the day to be patient, tolerant, understanding, and systematic; you can safely assume that much good will come of this.

239 The Ultimate Shift

It is extraordinary to witness people let go of their ego and let the God of their understanding work in their lives for the better of all.

It is exceptional to see people shift from reacting emotionally to responding in a reasonable manner, even under highly unfavorable circumstances.

It is amazing to become one of these people.

Are you living by your ego, or with a greater awareness of things outside of you? What is the measure of this for you today?

240 Instant Karma

Regardless of what you believe is next,

after this life,

do your best to be your best,

knowing that,

at the very least,

it will do some good, right here, right now.

No act is too small when it comes to bringing good into
the world. Make a difference.

241 Clear Your Mind

Quiet the noise of projection, and what do you hear?
Clear your mind of worry, and what do you see?
Settle yourself in faith, and what do you feel?

One by one, work with silence and calm; then take the
wisdom that arises from that sacred space and decide
what to do with the day.

242 Resentment

Resentment is an interesting thing. The more you let it build, the more it robs you of the very condition, hope, or relationship that you felt was threatened to begin with. Resentment is only a reaction, never the answer to your troubles.

Knowing this, choose to:
solve rather than stew,
wonder rather than worry,
and you will find the keys to moving through your discontent.

243 Your Biggest Fan

Be your own biggest advocate and champion.

Learn to observe, listen, question, challenge, encourage, plan, and execute, and you will have the greatest skills imaginable for closing the gaps in your goals and being of better service to others.

244 From the Heart

Speak from your heart; make love your language.

See from your heart; observe with a loving eye.

Laugh from your heart; cry from your heart; live from love.

Share your heart, just because you can.

Love because you must, because to love is the fullest expression of your soul.

In all things, let love be its own reward.

245 React or Respond

When you work hard to surround yourself with positive people, it can be especially jarring when someone is purposely unkind to you. It's easy to forget that sometimes people can be just plain mean.

When you're the target of unkindness, there are countless ways you could respond.

The most obvious recourse (and perhaps most likely for some folks) would be to strike back, to defend whatever position the other person is attacking.

Another option would be to ignore them all together, to simply write off the attack as their problem only.

Still another way to deal with an affront might be to consider their argument for any small shred of information that might be useful to how you show up in the future, and then to let the whole thing go.

You don't have to be completely passive nor altogether aggressive in the face of another's spite; you can choose another angle entirely, which is to reasonably examine their comments for any merit and draw whatever line of boundary you need to for any future interaction with them.

246 To Not Regret the Past

We are never fully separated from our past; it is a part of our memory bank, no matter how deeply hidden.

How it affects us is another matter, one which depends on how we've categorized the information.

If our past still threatens us, we must find power over it.

If it shames us, we must find power from or in it.

If it still makes us angry or resentful, we must find perspective, gratitude, and acceptance.

We never have to throw the past away, or pretend it didn't exist, but we would do well to put it in its proper, most useful place.

247 Negativity

There's nothing wrong with feeling negative emotions.

The problem is when we stay in negativity, wallowing in it, letting it create a film of despair and hopelessness.

If you can let negativity move you, spur you to action, and reenergize you to change for the better, you can transform it into a very powerful and beneficial stimulant.

248 Join the Conversation

Don't wait until you have the most perfect opinion, the quintessential diatribe on a subject, to join the conversation.

The most stimulating exchanges are those, which involve everyone's thoughts, questions, replies, and possibilities,

ones that demand we consider things from many angles, which challenge our capacity for curiosity,

which teach us to exchange perspectives and debate positions.

The best conversations are the ones that demand us to grow from them.

249 You

You have everything in the world to be proud of.

You are creative, loving, kind, funny, spirited, and smart.

You are determined, resourceful, and full of possibilities.

Spring from your strengths, recruit to your weaknesses, and create the pairing of talents that accomplishes extraordinary things.

250 Resolve

The reason we rarely follow through on resolutions made on a particular day is because we will only really commit to taking action when doing so is imperative, when the only thing that makes sense to meeting our goals is to push forward now.

When our old ways start to seriously bind and restrict us, we intuitively know it's time for a new set.

Our internal compass will drive us to follow through on what matters most, not some external calendar.

If the commitment and a special date coincide, hallelujah.

Most importantly, to foster resolve look for the best circumstances all around that make the decision the very best fit for you, whatever—and whenever—that decision may be.

251 Connection

When we disconnect from our solutions—mentors, community, Spirit, and service—we experience isolation like no other.

Plug in, and we are instantly reunited with this big, wonderful world, free once again to contribute, expand, and love.

The next time you're feeling low, remember: Resist that impulse to retreat into yourself, and reach out to your support system. It will lift your spirits faster than anything else ever could.

252 The Wise One

It is a wise person who understands that taking something personally doesn't have to entail overreacting emotionally. A very wise person, indeed.

Learn to take in difficult information without taking on negativity in the process.

253 To Dream

We know the importance of being in the now, and appreciating what is.

It is also important sometimes to totally let yourself go, to let your imagination run wild and envision amazing possibilities for your future.

Make right now one of those times you let loose, and love and appreciate the chance it gives you to dream.

254 Keep the Fire

How do you keep the fire alive for your passions in life?

Remember the effect you've had in the past, and what made you so effective.

Remember that you inspired, and how you were inspirational.

Remember that your lessons were lasting, and what made them so.

Remember these things, start fresh from these basics, and you will reignite your passion again and again.

255 Good Choices

It's not so hard to do something that's good for you.

The challenge is doing it again and again and again, sticking with it when it seems there's no progress or point, making it an integral part of your life and not quitting before the miracle.

The only way to do all these things is to make sure that the reason for your goal is bigger than any of your blocks or doubts.

And the way to do that is to revisit your "why" again and again, getting clearer and clearer on your motivation, and finding creative ways to stay mindful of it.

Pick a theme for your mission—a guiding word or phrase—and surround yourself with whatever notes and totems you need to remind you of its importance. If what you've written down doesn't hold up in the face of temptation, keep searching for the word or phrase that will.

256 Making a Shift

You don't have to go to external extremes to create internal shifts of identity; skydiving isn't the only way to feel adventurous.

One painting class could help you suddenly see yourself as creative.

One crucial conversation could help you finally feel brave.

One determined stand for something that deeply matters could fully reveal all the moxie you'll ever need.

Decide which identity you want to adapt or strengthen, engage wholeheartedly in an activity that aligns with it, and watch your newfound sense of confidence arise.

257 Choose Your Words

There is no lack of words, just the motivation to use them wisely.

Choose your words carefully and well, and you'll find just the right expression of your love, concern, curiosity, or joy.

258 Meeting Your Needs

We must learn to discern what we most need to be happy, healthy, stable, strong, spiritual, spirited, and the like.

These are the things we can direct when life storms around us, not the storms themselves.

And the best news is, we don't have to have all the answers, or go it alone; great progress comes from asking great questions in great company.

What would you say you really need to be happy, healthy, stable, strong, spiritual, spirited, and the like? What would your partner, your family, your friends say? Being clear on this will help you weather any storm.

259 Understand and Be Understood

No matter how hard you might try to make yourself understood, there will be people who hear only what they want to, who, upon discovering that you're not both on the same page, will make you so wrong that you can't help but wonder what else you could have said or done for a different outcome.

Fine-tuning your part in the conversation is exactly what you can do.

Improve how you outline your time frame and agenda;

clearly state whether you're seeking advice, consensus, or both;

and be willing to ask the same clarity of them,

all of which makes it highly likely that you will at least reach an understanding, if not actual agreement.

Through this process you're also highly unlikely to be held hostage to any disappointment that may arise—theirs or yours.

260 The Pain of Your Past

It is a vulnerable feeling, to be sure, to tell painful stories of your past.

And yet, in the telling, the energy transforms from one that, before, may have broken you down to one that helps you stand taller, stronger, more confident and aware; a charge that now moves you to tell your tale for the benefit of all.

Find strength in sharing your experience.

261 In Community

There is no more perfect place in which to be the change you want to see in the world than in a community that challenges you to stretch, grow, shift, change, and give back, just by your effort to be there, to contribute, and to learn.

That place could be anywhere people gather to share their experience, strength, and hope for some common purpose.

You can't effect great change all on your own. Commune with like-minded people again and again, and together you can shape a fantastically beneficial "new normal" for yourselves and those around you.

262 Inspiration

Inspiration is ever-present;

what you must appraise is how to overcome any obstacles—of mind, body, and spirit—that prevent you from

seeking,

creating,

inviting,

or receiving it.

There's no shortage of inspiration out there—we simply need to block out the distractions that prevent us from accessing it.

263 Your Story

The power in your story lies not so much in what you've overcome, but in how you've done so with dignity, grace, and compassion.

Live to tell your tale, and you will help more people than you know.

264 The Right Thing

There could be a million reasons why you think you should do something, but only a select few are the right ones.

Find the courage to stand for the select few.

265 Stepping Back

When someone you love is wrapped up in their own pain and confusion, forgets you're their ally, and lashes out at you in their pain, sometimes the best thing you can do is step away from them for a bit and let them sort out their own stuff alone.

As much as you'd like to, there are times when trying to help only makes matters worse.

As much as you fear they will suffer setbacks from their anguish, you have to give them room to learn from it.

As much as you worry whether the relationship will ever be restored, you must keep moving on your path with the faith that if you've tried your best to bring value to their lives that you will have helped in some way, on some level which you may or may not ever see, making you stronger and more useful to others as a result.

Sometimes the most loving thing we can do for a person is to step back and give them some space to grow.

266 Standing Firm

Sometimes the hardest thing to do in your own defense is not to argue or fight, but to do what seems like nothing at all:

Simply hold your ground.
Take all the negative energy away from the situation;
be peaceful with your stand and calm in your certainty,
no matter how much chaos swirls around you.

Have conviction in everything you do, knowing that you don't need to convert others or defend your beliefs.

267 Progress, not Perfection

Break free of the ego-driven, energy-sucking trap of
perfectionism;
let your soul instead be moved and lifted by
diligence,
creativity,
effectiveness,
and the chance to be helpful in all things.

There's no such thing as "perfection" anyway, only choices
that are right and beneficial.

268 Abundance

The first and best place to attract abundance is in your mind.

Be abundantly generous,
    kind,
    understanding,
    compassionate,
    curious,
    and humorous,

and it is likely that you will receive more (if not all) of the same.

If you want to receive abundance, give abundantly.

269 Learning from the Past

Every bit of your past can inform your present for the better, once you fully pay attention to how it can.

That doesn't mean life will be perfect once you're willing to take responsibility for your part in what happens, just that this practice will help you develop perfect clarity on how to influence your future for the better.

The great freedom is when you shun no piece of your story, when you can invite even the worst of it along as an important gauge of how much you've changed and grown.

270 Faith and Peace

If you can talk about faith but still feel like you've been forsaken, then stop talking about it and start doing something in faith.

If you can see exactly what others are going through but can't see that for yourself, stop looking at everyone else, and start looking at you.

If you can tell what advice anyone else could use but can't figure out what you need, stop offering help and start asking for it.

Pushing through our troubles and finding peace always involve moving from our minds to our hearts, leaving our intellectual understanding and connecting with and applying the wisdom that comes only from deep, personal experience.

271 In the Right Place

Maybe lost, but not alone.

Maybe alone, but not lonely.

Maybe lonely, but not unloved.

Maybe right where you need to be to decide where you want to go.

Find the gift in your circumstances, even if they don't feel totally ideal at the time.

272 Keeping Your Word

Being a person of your word doesn't mean you'll never make mistakes or act contrary to your values; it means you won't try to justify or ignore it when that happens.

As things change, as you change, what you value may change too, and it is critical that you be willing to examine and express what you can be counted on for, and what you cannot, no matter the consequences.

Keep your word, whatever it is.

273 It's Personal

The only way to take things, really, is personally, with your own views and judgments with which you filter everything you think you see.

The trick to keep from taking things *too* personally is to realize that everyone else is coming from a place of their own views and judgments as well, and that any negative expression of that from them isn't a personal affront, unless you decide to take it that way.

That's all quite personal, actually, which means you are 100 percent, personally in charge of whether or not you suffer at someone else's hands.

274 Making Assumptions

There are very few assumptions one can safely make without eventually suffering the disappointment of having a theory proved wrong by someone, somewhere.

Except the possibility of kindness, love, and compassion.

One can always assume that kindness, love, and compassion are possible when one assumes responsibility for manifesting them.

275 Self-Care

Self-care is not an all-at-once proposition. You've got lots of moving parts, after all.

First, state what you most want your life to be about emotionally, mentally, physically, spiritually, and financially.

Then do a quick assessment of how you feel about how your life is going in each of these categories, and hone in on what appears to need the most attention.

Finally, plan some actions that are in alignment with your expressed ideals.

With the action step revealed, all that remains then is for you to follow your own advice.

276 Being Cared For

Let yourself be cared for. Let those who love you see your pain, and let them help you better care for yourself in the process.

By all means, be choosy about who you share your struggles with. You know the difference between those who can't ever really be counted on to help you through the heavy stuff, and those who might not always be able to hold you up but who can always be counted on to try.

Choose the latter.

And know what "cared for" means for you, and state that up front.

"I need a shoulder right now."

"I need to say how I feel about something."

"I need to vent some frustrations."

Then let go of whether your confidante can respond or support you in any particular way; take comfort in the catharsis of speaking your truth, and be proud that you sought to be released from the negative emotions that bind you.

Regardless of whether you get the perfect answers from the perfect person at the perfect time, it is empowering to be vulnerable, to know that you have at least reached out on behalf of getting better.

277 Your Mission

You know your talents.
You know your strengths.
You know your values,
and you know your needs.
You also know your fears,
your hesitations,
and your blocks.

At the end of the day, you will either live in support of
what is comfortable and familiar, or you will go full out in
support of the most glorious version of your potential.

Either way, you'll still have fears. The quality of your
life will depend on the quality of your motivation to overcome those fears in support of a grander mission.

278 Speaking Up

If you hesitate to ever share what is really on your mind, you
will never get what you want, experience what you could, or
be of the type of service you might.

Sometimes you need to simply suck it up, breathe, and tell it like it is.

Yes, there are consequences for being so forthcoming.

But there are equally big ones for not being so bold.

You can be direct and honest without being loud or mean.

279 Coaching Others

It is an awesome gift when someone allows you to take a chance on them,

to coach them on how to express themselves more effectively and to see things from different angles;

to learn to negotiate conflict without losing their bearing;

to stay balanced and true to their values.

Chances are, you'll feel like you've gotten more from that relationship than you ever give.

A great reason to be mentored, coached, and taught great, deep lessons is for the tools and skills it gives you to support others in this way.

What an extraordinary way to pay things forward.

280 Back on Track

It's so easy to lose track of your goals and values, to lose your way. And when that happens, the frustration and anxiety of it can cloud your vision and keep you turning round and round, making you more and more uncertain of how to point yourself back in the right direction.

Stop.

Sit.

Rest.

Regroup.

Think about where you were trying to go. Think about how you strayed on the path, and why. Think about where it has led, and what might happen if you continue pushing on with no clear direction, tired, afraid, and alone.

Now, clear your mind, peacefully reconnect with your purpose and mission, get up, dust yourself off, and get going on whichever path you think will be most helpful, so that no matter where you end up, you will have had a most beautiful and impactful trip.

From time to time, check in on how things are going. Are you barreling ahead without clear direction? If so, it's time to regroup.

281 Starting Over

Love that you can start your day over as often as you need or want to,
that you can choose a new voice
of reason,
passion,
or imagination
to center and then move you.

Tomorrow is always a new day.

282 Stand Tall

Always stand in support of your highest and best use in the world.

Literally plant your feet, and connect with the great support of the earth beneath you.

As you ground yourself so, start to stretch and reach and lengthen your body and soul and spirit.

Be grounded in your convictions, tall and lifted in your aspirations.
There is no greater way to walk in the world.

283 Excellence

Excellence is not just a state of mind, it is planned for, deliberate, studied, copied, even assumed of oneself.

As you observe greatness in others, if you find that you're envious of their success, of their path to such a high standard of thought and action, first let go of your jealousy. Either study what they're doing and be willing to work as hard to get where they've gotten, or insist on reengaging at a higher level with your own goals and standards.

Either of these choices could lead you to most excellent results.

Plan how you'll be excellent today.

284 Abundance of Spirit

Abundance is not some external gift that one is bestowed, but an internal quality you generate by expanding your capacity to be more generous, kind, understanding, compassionate, curious, humorous, and loving.

Develop and express these qualities without reservation— particularly during the most difficult times, with the most challenging people—and you will know an abundance of spirit like no other.

285 What If?

What if you let go, for one day, of having to be super knowledgeable?

What if you approached some things as though you were seeing, hearing, and experiencing them for the first time?

What if you asked more questions and made fewer statements?

What if you set out to enjoy the day, completely open to what it might bring?

What if, in all this curiosity, you found the missing link of information that, once known, would truly launch the next chapter of your life?

Well?

Embrace the uncertain; appreciate the unknown; let go of having to know and control for today.

286 Confidence

We need to hold ourselves to a higher standard of emotional stability and confidence.

We need to claim our rightful place in the world.

We need to trust the world's infinite capacity to support our brilliance, sincerity, and love.

We need to teach others to do the same.

Because we can and it matters.

Act with certainty, knowing that you've thought through your feelings and determined the best course for you.

287 Handling Crisis

No matter how difficult a situation may be, take time to hone the skills, pull the focus, and find the faith that will get you through it.

A well-executed to-do list can be as enlightening and uplifting as prayer if it keeps you moving forward in spite of your pain.

Being so practical in the face of emotional turmoil doesn't mean you don't care; it just shows that you can be conscientious in a crisis, which may be just the bit of confidence you need to make it through another day.

Breaking a crisis down into smaller steps makes it easier to manage. Take time to breathe, think, and then act.

288 Evolve

It's never too late to make a new contract with yourself, a promise based on choosing that which promotes spiritual growth in you and others, even when that choice is so painful that you're tempted to revert to behavior that only serves your baser needs.

It's never too late to grow.

289 Conscious Awareness

Some people are born with a heightened sense of awareness of themselves and the world around them, and how one affects the other.

Most, however, need to consciously hone this skill, which simply comes with practice; you develop greater awareness by practicing greater awareness any time, place, or way that you can.

There are many guides for practice—your five senses, for instance.

Spend time getting in touch with what you see, smell, taste, hear, and touch throughout the day, and find a greater understanding of how that shapes your thoughts, perspectives, and actions.

Or pay close attention to your physical being, to how you literally take up and move through space, and how that affects you and others, positively or negatively.

You can also become more mindful of your emotions, looking at what they are, where they come from, and how you express them, for better or for worse.

Practicing conscious awareness is a process, a constant molding of our instincts and understanding with an eye for how to better ourselves and be more helpful to one another.

It keeps us from crashing into each other, literally and figuratively, which is a very good thing.

290 Self-Will

Where there is a will, there is a way to talk ourselves into
all sorts of people, places, and things that seem like exactly
what we need in that moment,
>   when one extra beat,
>   one simple pause
>   could reveal what's really best all around.

Patience makes room for true insight.

291 Breathe

There are times in life that are so hard all you can do is
breathe. (And sometimes even that feels hard.)
>   If you give that breath a chance, it settles everything—
>   your mind,
>   your body,
>   your racing heart—
>   and it creates more and more space for serenity, peace,
and ease.
>   Breathe in as deeply as you can, hold it in for just a few
seconds, then let it out with a whoosh.
>   Do it again.
>   And again.
>   There, doesn't that feel better?

Don't underestimate the power of the breath.

292 Faith

Having faith doesn't mean that if we sit and do "this," then "that" will simply come to us.

Rather, faith should nudge us constantly forward, ever so patiently reminding us to fully engage in being more useful each day.

This faith in what to do (regardless of what we get) doesn't take away the bumps in the road, but it does give us a keen sense of purpose with which to keep moving and growing on the path, making the journey its own wondrous reward.

Have faith; believing in something will make you happier, healthier, and more joyful.

293 Personal Growth

To really "own" your part in something means that you must be willing to ask for and receive feedback on your behavior, go beyond an intellectual understanding of the information and truly examine it for its merits (particularly the parts that are the hardest to hear), and be willing to develop strategies—thoughts, words, actions—for change.

This is true in good times and in bad, for better or for worse. We can be just as resistant to praise as to criticism.

This progression, this willingness to work deeply with the information at hand, is your golden opportunity to have your character defects replaced with qualities that serve a higher purpose.

Pretty simple, definitely not so easy, but oh-so-worth the work.

294 Take It Easy

If you have a spare moment today, take it.

> Take it to reflect,
> to rest,
> to appreciate,
> to love.

Make time for appreciating the world around you.

295 Happiness

If we define ourselves and our happiness by whom and what
we are
    attached to,
    loved by,
    seen with,
    and so forth,
we will always be on shaky emotional and spiritual ground,
due to the impermanence of all people, places, and things.

Instead, let us ground ourselves in the everlasting principles
of love and compassion.
    Let these be the solid footing on which we stand,
the source of our ultimate fulfillment and peace.

**True happiness comes from within, from knowing and
having love and compassion.**

296 Be Brave

It's a great day to be brave,
to smile in the face of adversity,
to honor your commitments,
and to take the small actions that will help you stretch and
grow.

As you're facing the challenges of the world today, chin
up. Be brave.

297 To Learn

Today is a great day for conscious intelligence, to engage
in learning that takes you to new and exciting places, and
conversations that challenge and provoke you; ones that
even require you to do a little homework, perhaps, in order
to keep up.

It's a great day to stretch your brain.

298 That's Life

Life doesn't know that you have expectations.

It's not out to get you,

or timing its blows.

But things are not completely random, either. So be careful what you make of things, the parallels you draw between one thing and the next, because you wouldn't want to create and perpetuate a negative story.

Life is what we make of it, thought-to-thought, day-by-day.

299 Have, Want, and Need

In life, there is

what we can have

what we really want,

and what is most beneficial.

The trick of a happy life is to close the distance between these three.

300 Playful and Wise

If we just let our to-do lists, planning, and projecting run the show, we are likely to be left feeling that we've done a bunch of stuff but not really accomplished anything at the end of the day.

> But when we remember to let
> our intuition be at play,
> our insight to arise,
> and our faith to guide us,
> we are playful, and wise, and sure of our path,
> and certain to find fulfillment and joy.

Make time today to play. After all, what's the point of work if there's no play?

301 A New Approach

Just for today,
replace anxiety with awareness,
worry with wonder,
and overwhelm with loving, discerning detachment.

You are bound to have plenty of opportunities for practice, for which you can be grateful rather than peeved.

302 Build Your Network

To be successful in any area of your life, it's not necessary that you have all the answers, all by yourself.

On the contrary, your best asset for reaching your goals is the confidence that you either know your answers or know where to get them, which comes from building a network of experts, friends, and associates on whom you can call at any given moment to advance what you do know, and to fill in the blanks of what you don't.

Confident, successful people aren't 100 percent sure of anything 100 percent of the time, except perhaps of their capacity to ask for help and expand their resources.

303 Come Alive

Allow yourself to really come alive today, to wake the creative, playful, determined, and spirited energies so crucial to your well-being, those which may have lain dormant while you tended to other things.

Paint, dance, sing, write, imagine, dream, pray.

Tend these seats of your soul, and you will never be at a loss for the energy and enthusiasm for life that makes you such a great force for good in the world.

304 The Business of Life

Take special care of the "business" of your life, the systems for health, wealth, comfort, and safety that support your greater good.

Get organized, informed, situated, complete, aware—whatever it takes for you to operate at maximum speed and benefit.

Start by seeing this not as a bunch of boring tasks, but as elements of your ultimate success. For example, see balancing your checkbook as critical to fostering abundance; physical health keeps you strong, alert, and ready for new opportunity; a clean and tidy home provides the perfect sanctuary in which to dream and plan the future.

305 Thoughtfulness

Tame your mind,
condition it to wander thoughtfully in imagination of
a better, more purposeful future
and limitless, positive possibility,
rather than allowing it to race to negative conclusions that
terrorize you with baseless fear.

Whatever comes up, apply hope over fear.

306 Joyful

Be joyful today
over nothing in particular.

Bask in the great energy of faith and gratitude,
and be more ready, willing, and able than ever
to do the next, right, beautiful thing,
whatever that may be.

An open heart is a joyful heart.

307 Self-Improvement

We are different—
better, stronger, more focused, more loving, and more
helpful—
when we agree to mind our conduct for more than our own
sake.

It's not an easy task, acting for others as well as ourselves,
and we're not perfect at it (sometimes we're not even that
great at it).

But we always know, at least in the end, that this commitment is always worth it.

308 Being Direct

Constantly work to hone the elements—
the statements, questions, and challenges—
for asserting yourself in a more honest, forthright, respectful, in-the-moment manner.

It's no small task, deconstructing old habits of communication and building anew, yet press on, faithful that doing so
will lead to some greater end.

309 Accessibility

Being available to others, in service to your sense of purpose
and mission, doesn't require that you sacrifice your well-
being to be effective.

You don't have to run yourself ragged in support of your
ideals: You can schedule your accessibility and balance "me"
time with social time so that you don't neglect yourself in
the process of helping others.

You don't have to be all things to all people, either.
There is such a thing as being hypersensitive to others'
needs, which creates enormous and undue stress. The

moment we stop asking "Who can help the most?"—being open to all possibilities—is the moment we put more pressure on ourselves than we need to be most effective.

We don't have to have all the answers. Rather, we should strive to have enough connections with experts of all stripes that we can easily be someone's guide instead of trying to be their guru.

310 Adaptability

It's funny to look at how set in our ways we can be. Sure, we say we're open-minded, but how often do we allow ourselves to test that theory?

When a situation arises that demands that you adapt to new systems, strategies, philosophies, or personalities, what is your first feeling?

Are you curious or skeptical?

Excited or afraid?

Resistant or willing to give it a go?

The answer is probably a combination of all of the above.

At the end of the day, understand that all cells of your being don't have to instantly adapt to something new; it can be equally beneficial to be strategic in your newfound flexibility, to test a new idea or scenario first in your mind, and imagine your plans B, C, and D should things not work out according to how you supposed.

In any case, don't let your habits of mind stop you from setting new ways of thinking, speaking, and acting, which starts with a willingness to be open to suggestion and flexible to change.

311 Being Prosperous

Prosperity is not something to be taken in the abstract; prosperity simply is.

It is something you choose.

It is something you accept.

It is something you prove in fact, not theory, be it by your health, wealth, property, or prestige.

It is something you embrace, celebrate, and share; it has no value as a solo venture.

It is something that, by its very definition, is to be "of means."

The means to do what and for whom is up to you.

Use this as your guide to living a prosperous life.

312 Ride the Waves

You can't avoid the stormy waves of life, but you can learn
to relax and work with them, to let them carry you to a new
and better place.

Let disappointment take you to gratitude.

Let scorn take you to compassion.

Let fear take you to faith,
loss to recovery,
and uncertainty to hope.

**The waves may knock you around, but they needn't take
you under.**

313 Happy Being

A new beginning is no guarantee of a happy ending;
better to strive for a happy daily being,
one that helps you grow in love and usefulness.
For then, no matter how many painful and joyful twists and
turns you take along the way,
the journey will have been worth it.

**Life is more about the journey than the perfect, happy
ending. So enjoy each day for what it is.**

314 Tell the Truth

Do everything it takes to maintain the integrity of your relationships, to live up to your commitments, regardless of where they may ultimately end up.

In particular, tell the truth to that person—be it a friend, business associate, or romantic partner—whom it affects the most.

There is no guarantee of how the information will be received, only the assurance that in continuing to communicate, even when it's the most difficult thing to do, regardless of the outcome, you can take comfort in knowing you've been true to your standard of honesty.

The truth will not only set you free, it may just be what's needed to free another.

315 Be Amazing

What would it take for you to be amazing,
or joyful,
or bold,
or sensational,
or any other word you'd really like to describe you?

Could it be as simple as deciding to be?

316 To Share or Not to Share

There is no such thing as being too honest, only in being so blunt in your delivery that others can't get past their shock to really hear what you're saying, much less find the willingness to act on it for anyone's benefit.

The key to candor that fosters a deep and helpful exchange is motive.

Motive speaks louder than content: Only share when you mean to be constructive.

Once you know what you want to share, and why, use that information to frame your conversation, to help others prepare to engage: "I'd like to share my (observation/concern/opinion/impression) for the sake of helping (fill in the blank)."

Let compassionate intention and a clear framework inform a soft, yet determined style of communication, and you will at least have laid the groundwork for productive dialogue.

317 Cleverness

If someone tells you that you're clever, they may not necessarily mean it as a compliment.

Without the right motives, the ability to think on your feet and sidestep any real troubles may only prove you're more cunning than cooperative.

When you're feeling oh-so-clever (especially if there is even a hint of smugness that goes with the feeling), be willing to examine whether you're driving things more for comfort than for impact, in a way that is out of line with what you truly stand for.

If you find that you're guilty of that, go through the searching and fearless process of taking inventory and making amends for the situation, and you will find relief—for you and others—from the bondage of this particular selfishness, this particular time.

This doesn't mean you'll never be selfish again; it means you will have raised your awareness and strengthened your willingness to be less and less so, making you more and more effective overall.

And aren't you grateful for the tools to examine your blind spots, calmly accept the truth of what you see, and strengthen your character as a result?

318 Procrastination

There's a big difference between being "done" and being "finished."

"Done" is the state of having completed something to a level of satisfaction that might still have room for improvement, yet is perfectly acceptable for the desired impact.

"Finished" may just be the same trap of the mind as "perfect," a state which only makes us put off what must be done because we need to get it just so before it's "enough."

Enough with the procrastination and word games, already. Do your thing, do it as best you can, and do it as soon as you can to help the most people.

Nobody said this would be the last word on whatever the subject is from you anyway, right?

319 Progress, not Perfection

We're supposed to be in the now, but look, there go our minds, running from the past and racing to the future.

We're supposed to take personal responsibility for our actions, and not worry about whether others are doing so, but look, there we go taking someone else's inventory.

We're supposed to develop a relationship with a higher power of our own understanding, but look, there we go resisting the relationship.

We're supposed to raise our awareness of our thoughts and our conduct, but there we go getting bogged down in old, limiting habits and beliefs.

What a process, all this pushing and pulling, coming and going, striving and faltering.

Look, there we go being human.

320 Great Expectations

Take a look at the progress in your life, at how much more people now expect of you, because of how much you have improved in one area or another.

Higher standards bring higher expectations of our conduct, no doubt, but would you want to live any other way?

Is there any better pressure than to live an examined, purposeful life, full of mistakes and lessons and triumphs and trials, at once magnificent and messy?

Would you trade that for anything?

321 Patience

You can't be everyone's guide to happiness.

Actually, you rarely get to see exactly how or when something you've said or done has positively impacted someone.

You have to be patient and remember that everyone is on their own path, and that their journey to peace and freedom will take whatever amount of time it takes. You have no power over its twists and turns, only the potential to influence how rough the road.

Know that if your intent is to be helpful, you have been, on some level, seen or unseen;

know that you're setting an example that could have a wholly different impact than you can even imagine;

and know that by being helpful, you're doing what you're supposed to, regardless of the outcome.

Just be patient.
That too is helpful.

322 Scattered

When you have just too many things swirling around you— so many things to think about and take care of that you can't even finish a thought, much less a task— step back, get a fresh piece of paper, and gather your thoughts by writing out the guiding principles that are most important to you.

Then look at your day, and decide how to act in support of your principles, in whichever category of your life you choose.

Don't worry about whether you can do this with everything, do it for life, or even do it tomorrow.

Do it just for today, for whatever you can.

323 Celebration

So many victories, so many ways to celebrate, right here, right now.

Do a little dance,

Sing a little song.

Write a little poem.

Talk to a friend.

High-five yourself.

Don't let the moment pass without a little bit of a party.

324 Quietude

Every once in awhile, plan to make your way quietly through the day, to be very present to what comes up from the noiselessness.

You don't have to turn off all technology; the goal is to be quiet, not unplugged, and to only engage in conversation that is productive, fulfilling, and impactful.

As Gandhi once encouraged us, "Speak only if it will improve upon the silence."

As you practice mindful silence and directed speech, you will create more space than ever for intuition, imagination, and insight to arise.

325 Destiny

Perhaps it's not that everything happens for a reason, as though each experience is "meant" to teach us a predetermined lesson, but rather that if we're willing to look for it, we will find reason in everything that happens.

Don't make destiny condescend to being obvious; pick up on its subtle cues.

326 Right Work

Find your way to work that feeds your soul and promotes your ability to better serve in this world.

Your livelihood may be the direct route to making an impact—perhaps your calling has become your career.

It may also be that your work provides the means—the money, schedule, or connections—that support a mission outside of your job.

Either way, do everything you can to see to it that your time spent working is in some way bettering you for the sake of whom you can serve.

We spend more than half our lives in our respective jobs; it's up to each of us to find meaning in or through them.

327 Guilt

It's one thing to feel guilty because you did something you knew you shouldn't have. In that case, make amends and move on.

It's quite another to feel remorseful over the consequences of your actions, for which you can make amends and restitution, and then move on.

If you're just disappointed that the choices you make to support your highest good put you at odds with others, then maybe it's sadness you feel, not guilt.

In any case, own your choices and the emotions proportionate to the circumstances, and then move on.

328 Anticipation

Make plans.

Put the wheels in motion.

Prepare for a positive outcome.

Anticipate what you will say, feel, and do.

Get excited by the possibilities.

Make room for additional or alternative possibilities.

Enjoy the experience, whatever the outcome.

Celebrate what worked.

Acknowledge what didn't.

Let it all inform the future.

329 Relating

How magnificent, to have people in your life with whom you can share your stories, fears, and dreams.

People who will actively listen, who want to learn who you are through what and how you relate, who challenge you to stretch and grow, and who share an appreciation for life's eccentricities.

We rarely find all of these skills in one person in our lives; typically there are bits of each of these gifts in many different folks.

Some people are better listeners than others; some are natural problem solvers; some are simply and perfectly content to hear your voice, no matter what.

Celebrate these people and the qualities of communication that bond your relationship, and you will never be at a loss for companionship.

330 Being Alone

We say we don't want to be alone.

Rather, we don't want to be lonely.

There are plenty of times that we want to be by ourselves, just not completely on our own, with no one else to depend on.

We crave the company of others, which is fine as long as our internal happiness and security isn't dependent upon this external connection; because at times you will be the only one you can turn to and count on.

In those times when you feel completely left to your own devices, you will still draw on the wisdom of countless people who have influenced you in the past to see you through your present challenge.

You never have to be alone; it's a choice, not a mandate.

331 Giving

In giving—of our time, talent, and treasures—we get to do
so many things:
make an impact,
practice nonattachment,
be part of a bigger picture,
join a community,
apply our faith.

In giving, we get so much more than we give.

332 Honor

You become a person of honor when you practice honor.

Embrace the lessons of your past and your present.

Gladly give the glory of your accomplishments to others.

Graciously accept the accolades you are given.

Be counted on to do what's fair and right.

Develop a reputation for integrity.

See the opportunities of this precious human existence as
a privilege, not a right.

333 Never Hold Back

Never hold back on saying or doing what might help another.

Afraid the words have already been said, and the actions already taken?

You are unique—in your tone, pace, inflection, intent, movement, drive, and passion. No one has your special way of thinking, saying, and doing things, so speak up and put yourself out there to make a difference in a way only you can.

You will never regret putting your special talents to work for the greater good when you're more driven by impact than style.

334 The Voice of Reason

The next time you're stressed, imagine this conversation parlayed in your head in whoever's voice—parent, friend, Spirit—you imagine to be most supportive and least judgmental.

You: "That's not what I intended."

Them: "What did you intend?"

You: "I'm not sure."

Them: "How will you be sure of your intentions next time?"

You: "I will think before I speak and act."

Them: "Great plan."

Give yourself a break. Odds are, most of your mistakes will be able to be remedied, if you can just gain clarity.

335 Tuning In

There is hardly a more fulfilling state than feeling in tune with another, this harmonious interaction that vibrates at such an optimum frequency that you are each able to send and receive crystal clear messages and music of the mind and soul.

You can't push or demand this most exquisite of connections; you must patiently make room for it, invite it, and, most importantly, honor it once it is established.

It is so worth the time.

336 Express Yourself

Don't assume that how you express yourself is enough to carry the message others need to hear.

At work, don't end the conversation with your willingness to take on a project or role; take the next step of sharing your enthusiasm for its potential impact, as in, "I'm excited to take this on because of . . ." instead of only saying, "Yes, I'll do this."

At home, don't take the excitement and affection of your friends and family for granted; let them know—frequently, and with gusto—just how much they mean to you and the difference they've made in your life.

The portrait of your life—who you are, how you feel, and where you stand—is yours to paint.

337 Chill Out

As much as we may try, it can be difficult to regulate the intensity at which we operate each day.

Sometimes our minds and bodies have to step in and do it for us, shut us down through sickness and exhaustion.

But as we become more and more mindful of balancing our energy and pace each day—as we learn to stop and smell the roses, as it were—we find our bodies don't have to go to such extremes to remind us to chill out.

We may still hit a wall from time to time, but with this awareness it gets a little softer—feels more like foam, maybe, than brick—the more we consciously take time to play and rest and regroup.

338 Love

Love is love: It is not created or guaranteed by our social constructs, and when we insist on defining love by our relationship frameworks, we risk corrupting and diminishing its purity and power.

Let our unions be a sacred space in which to honor love, celebrate love, express and experience and share love, whatever those unions may be.

339 Life Changes

When we make a significant shift in our careers or relationships, it can feel for a time like we're on the edge of a new life, when truly—the moment we decide to make the shift—we're smack in the middle of it, waiting for perhaps nothing more than the certainty that the path we're choosing is the right one, which we can't know right away.

Seeds sown take time to sprout, much less bloom, so the best we can do with these monumental decisions is put our hearts in the right place from the start.

Check your motives and choose based on what will make you of greatest benefit to all.

Having the right intention may be the hardest step we take, but it is what starts us off on the right path of whichever journey we choose.

340 Clear Vision

People in our day-to-day lives do a better job of telling us
where they're coming from than we often give them credit for.

If we will simply open our eyes, ears, and hearts to
what they're saying and doing—without the filter of our
expectations—we will see whether who they are, what they
want, and how they behave is a fit for our own needs and can
choose our next steps accordingly.

Don't condemn others for how they choose to move about
the world; simply learn to discern whether it serves to
move about with them.

341 Making Your Needs Known

Here's a simple framework for stating your wishes: "I'd like
to spend X amount of time doing Y for the sake of Z. Does
that work for you?"

Not complicated, essentially it paints a very clear picture of what you want.

What it does require is forethought. You and those
to whom you express your desires deserve to know what
you're after, and the best time to articulate that is before you
engage, not once you're in the middle or at the end of things.

If you don't know what you want, say that: "I'd like to
spend X amount of time exploring Y to see what comes of it."

If the other person is in agreement, you now have a structure and shape for the interaction that frees everyone to work more efficiently toward a clear outcome.

All it takes to make your needs known in this way is a little bit of practice, for which the day always provides countless opportunities.

342 Good Judgment

It doesn't matter how you got the know-how for assessing a situation and determining the most beneficial response to it; what matters is that you exercise that judgment, and that you practice reason and logic until you are savvy to the core.

Learn to think things through—all the way through, not just as far as you're comfortable with.

Imagine the what-ifs of the many angles before you. Try on different scenarios and outcomes in your mind to find which would be most beneficial.

And once you've examined the situation and its possibilities, take action.

With a little bit of intuition, a dash of discernment, and a rash of reckoning and prudence, you will develop the wisdom and insight that will help you mold a greatly fulfilling life.

343 Spontaneity

Spontaneity is a beautiful trait when it carries the qualities of being unrehearsed, relaxed, and open in your communication, and free and easy in your approach to things.

It can be tricky—even dangerous—when it manifests as impulsiveness, that weird insistence on getting what you want when you want it, karma be damned.

At the core of both is your awareness of cause and effect: Do you look to it for guidance and wisdom, or turn a blind eye to it in favor of reckless abandon?

Spontaneity and impulsiveness are not without thought. Choose wisely, in either case.

344 Caring for Stuff

Caring for your material stuff plays a major part in creating an environment that supports your highest good.

Unclutter your space; unclutter your mind.
Organize your stuff; organize your thoughts.

Dust and shine and display precious mementos with a mind toward highlighting your gifts, accomplishments, and values.

Create a comfortable, peaceful sanctuary that invites the contemplation and rest you need to be physically, emotionally, mentally, and spiritually at your best.

But beware of crossing over the line into materialism—caring for your things is something you do to support the bigger picture of your life; caring about things—as in getting overly attached to them—is a trap that narrowly defines you and stifles your growth.

345 Balance

A balanced life isn't something you schedule, it is a way of being: inside and out; mind, body, and soul; every chance you get.

Balance your mind; be more present.

Balance your speech; be more thoughtful.

Balance your approach; be more about "we," less about "me."

Balance your movement; be more active or settled, as needed.

Balance your priorities; be more engaged than just busy.

Balance your objectives; be more interested in influence than control.

Balance your emotions; be more calm.

Just look at all the balance you can achieve when you decide to.

346 No Worries

All worry fades when you put your heart in the right place of compassion, service, and faith.

There's no room to be agitated when you practice compassion.

There's no room for personal apprehension when you serve others.

There's no room for fear when you exercise faith.

347 Know It All

You've heard it all, everything you ever need to be healthy and happy.

There are no new words; only new combinations of words that may help you finally break through the darkness to find the light in your life.

So keep reading, watching, digging, searching for truth and meaning, and you will find it.

It doesn't matter if you've heard it all before;
keep listening.

348 Your Reputation

How you are seen

isn't created in one day or one week or one month;

isn't based on one person's opinion;

isn't formed by one incident.

Your reputation is a culmination of countless impressions you make based on how you respond to the demands of your life, day in and day out.

Some days will be better than others; no one is perfect.

To be seen in the best possible light, you must have a higher-than-average commitment to matching your words and actions to the best possible intentions.

No matter what your reputation is today, you can instantly impact it for the better by diligently working to close the gap between how you are and how you hope to be every chance you get today.

A stellar reputation that "precedes you by a week" takes a bit longer than that to build.

349 Morning Inventory

Inventory tends to be thought of as a process of looking back on certain circumstances, analyzing what worked and what didn't for the situation, and owning our part in the results (hopefully celebrating the victories and making amends for any shortcomings).

There is also such a thing as a "forward inventory," and morning is the perfect time for it. Look first at whether you need to cleanse yourself of any negativity, stress, worry, assumptions, or resentments that could make for a difficult day, and replace them with a dedication to act with positivity, generosity, compassion, and kindness.

Of course, there's an ongoing opportunity to check in and see what still needs to be cleared throughout the day.

With this much conscious conduct in a day, there should be much more to celebrate than to make up for.

350 Taking a Leap

When you're contemplating making major changes in your life, remember that no one just pops into the air from where they are and lands somewhere new and fabulous.

There are lots of little steps to consider before you jump into something new.

Taking a leap of faith still requires a running start.

351 Divine Coincidence

Divine coincidence: the exquisite, extraordinary, not wholly unexpected meeting of minds and missions across lifetimes and miles, connecting purpose with passion; becoming the fit to each other's dreams in ways previously unimagined but certainly hoped for.

This sublime intersection of souls takes intention, a willingness to inconvenience oneself for some greater good.

It also takes intuition, an ability to identify the best parts of one's character and talents to put in play.

And it most definitely takes faith, a certainty that being a conduit for possibility and impact attracts like-minded souls and circumstances.

Simply put, divine coincidence occurs when we make room for the Divine.

352 "Branding"

Your professional brand is your appeal, the qualities about you that make people want to engage with you and avail themselves of your talents.

Which begs the question, what are your qualities and talents, and do they support your future ambitions, and those of your company?

Ask yourself what you currently bring to the relationship—is it innovation, follow-through, peace of mind, technical expertise?

It may be all those things and more; what's key is to identify and nurture those existing qualities, while discovering and developing the additional skills that are needed to best meet the demands of your environment, particularly if you want to continue to climb the ladder of success.

If you don't know what is or isn't working with your "brand," ask for feedback from those whose support is most helpful.

Once you've decided what you want your brand to be, the process of marketing that brand means taking every opportunity to put those skills in play for the greater good; not as a way to say "look at me," but for the sake of sharing best practices.

Why brand yourself? Because it's happening already, whether you know it or not, with the impressions you make each day, and your future success depends on making it a conscious process.

353 Envy

There may be no greater waste of time than envy.

We need to stop wishing and hoping and coveting, and either do what it takes to get what we want, or let go of the desire.

Enough said.

354 One Shot

We get one shot at this life—not one shot in it—to do what moves us, matters to us, makes us proud of how we've lived.

Your time is now, while you're reading this. Decide what shots to take that will forever alter the enormously positive difference you can make in the world.

Who knows if we get another shot at another life after this one; let's go for the gusto with the one we've got.

355 Innovation

Here's how to be innovative:

Say, "I've got an idea, why don't we . . ." and follow that up with a creative, fresh twist on an old method, system, thought process, or routine.

Some people have even gone on to great careers or lifestyle shifts simply by their willingness to look for novel ways to approach things, without necessarily trying to reinvent the wheel.

Just see what's possible if you shake things up a bit.

356 The Power of Karma

You can't deny the laws of cause and effect; there is just too much evidence to support the theory.

Sooner or later, results will manifest from your actions.

You may not be the one who suffers or benefits from them, but someone will someday, in this generation or the next.

You have an effect on everything you touch.
Make it matter.

357 Setting Boundaries

The key to setting strong personal boundaries is to be sure enough of your values in all categories of your life that you can simply say no to what isn't a fit for them, unless you find, through careful consideration, that it makes sense to flex that boundary.

You'll know if it makes sense to be flexible if you're not compromising your effectiveness or sense of inner peace and happiness to do so.

Establish your own boundaries—left to someone else's devices, you risk living with parameters that aren't a fit for you at all.

358 Be Real

We put things into neat little packages sometimes, tell the hard stories of our life as though they were as devoid of emotion then as they are now in the telling.

We're afraid to be vulnerable, to tell the truth of how things affect us, lest the naming of them enables their permanent rule over us.

We really know better than that.

We know that things affect us on a deep emotional level, and it's important to accurately identify the feelings that arise accordingly.

How else will we bring those emotions into enough light to see them as the temporary confusions they really are, with no more weight or consequence than we allow?

To look at our emotions in this way is not to deny them, but to have the ultimate say in what future role they might play.

359 Obsession

Obsession is nothing more than the preoccupation caused by a lack of confidence in a choice.

Once you make the right decision, obsession lessens and then leaves.

That doesn't mean you'll never think about your choice again, just that you will have gained so much clarity by your willingness to do the right thing that there will be little to no room left for worry.

You will be at peace.

You know you've made the right decision when it seems easy and natural. If you are antagonized by a decision you've made, if you're obsessed, it's time to change course.

360 Spirit Guides

Be alert to who will be your guide on earth today,

through whose eyes you will take a new and improved look at the world and your place in it.

That guide may be human or animal, on earth or on high, real or imagined.

It will reveal itself in due time, once you make yourself available to it.

Who do you imagine your spirit guide to be?

361 A Friend in Need

One of the greatest gifts imaginable is friends who can acknowledge your present-day pain while sharing their vision of how your particular gifts and strengths will carry you through it, not as a blue-sky way of protecting you or making you temporarily feel better, but based on what they really know you're capable of.

These are the ones who connect with your pain rather than commiserate over it; who see the immediate needs created by the crisis—a meal, a drive, a compassionate ear, and the like—and look to help you feel those needs.

Be that friend. Be the person your friends turn to in times of need. Be the one they can trust to be sincere and supportive.

362 Have a Heart

Set your heart on love,
wear it proudly on your sleeve,
and never, ever, let relative rejection, disappointments, or temporary setbacks prevent you from channeling this most powerful and moving force for good.

Seek love with an open heart, and you're sure to find it.

363 Security

Sometimes the most enlightening place to be is alone with your insecurities, forced to confront them, to wool them around in your mind like a dog with an old blanket, until you are ready to set them down in favor of some more useful thought process.

As much as you'd like to, you can't run from your insecurities or deny them outright, because everywhere you go, there you are, as are they.

And there, too, is this unseen (and sometimes forgotten) source that wants what's best for you and is a champion for your confidence and happiness.

So stay put, set your doubts aside, reconnect with your faith in Spirit, and soon you will be ready to rejoin the world at large.

364 Give Thanks

To the family, friends, and strangers who give you
solace,
encouragement,
sanctuary,
smiles,
hugs,
laughter,
compassion,
guidance,
and love,
give thanks.
As you overcome your fears,
follow your heart,
and strive to be your best,
give thanks.
Now and forever.

Amen.

365 Wisdom

Wisdom is innate, born in us, pure and unadulterated when we arrive, inherent to all beings.

How well we cultivate it, and to what end we apply it—for good or for evil—is our individual choice, every instance of every day.

The wisest and most beneficial thing you can do is to ask yourself, "What is the wisest course of action I can take for the better?" and then act upon what arises from that inquiry.

Your answers will come, and if you are still and open-minded, you will intuitively know how to choose most wisely.

Acknowledgments

While this book is a compilation of lessons I've learned throughout my life, it was written during a particularly difficult period, one of great grief, transition, and growth. It would not have been possible to complete this manuscript were it not for the emotional, spiritual, and sometimes literal refuge provided by some of my dearest friends: Steve Donelson, Tania Oryshchyn, Debbie Phillips, Jill Siegel, Ann Vertel, Brandy and Dan Bertram, Stacey and Brendan Landry, Dave Frederick, Alecia Huck, and Gail Richards.

For that matter, the book would not have had its start were it not for the faith and trust of my erstwhile mentor, fellow author Karen Casey, who introduced me to my publisher, the ever-so patient, grounded, and visionary Jan Johnson. My deepest gratitude to you both for your belief in me and my work.

Nothing great in my life has happened without the unflagging support and love of my family: Mom (Karen), Butch, Janet, Katy, Tom, Deb, John, Tracy, Chris, Ruth, J.B., Desiree, Callum, Aiden, Taylor, Logan, Lauren, and Evan, you've all played a part in keeping me focused on doing what I love for the sake of whom I might serve. My love for you knows no bounds.

And finally, to my Dad: I owe you so much, not the least of which is my love of the written word, and my dedication to using my writing to help another. I miss you more every day, and know you'd be proud of my work.

Index

About the Author

 Jenifer Madson is an award-winning author, speaker, and success coach whose journey in recovery from addiction has informed every aspect of her work in the personal development field. She coaches and mentors people from all walks of life—from at-risk youth to Fortune 100 executives—on how to awaken to their highest potential. She lives in New York City, and when she's not writing or teaching, she can be found in the dance studio, on a motorcycle, or in a 12-step meeting. Visit her at *www. jenifermadson.com.*

To Our Readers

Conari Press, an imprint of Red Wheel/Weiser, publishes books on topics ranging from spirituality, personal growth, and relationships to women's issues, parenting, and social issues. Our mission is to publish quality books that will make a difference in people's lives—how we feel about ourselves and how we relate to one another. We value integrity, compassion, and receptivity, both in the books we publish and in the way we do business.

Our readers are our most important resource, and we appreciate your input, suggestions, and ideas about what you would like to see published.

Visit our website at *www.redwheelweiser.com* to learn about our upcoming books and free downloads, and be sure to go to *www.redwheelweiser.com/newsletter* to sign up for newsletters and exclusive offers.

You can also contact us at *info@rwwbooks.com*.

Conari Press
an imprint of Red Wheel/Weiser, LLC
665 Third Street, Suite 400
San Francisco, CA 94107